Book 9

LIBERATION

The Dutch in Wartime
Survivors Remember

Edited by

Anne van Arragon Hutten

Mokeham Publishing Inc.

© 2013 Mokeham Publishing Inc.
Box 20203, Penticton, B.C., V2A 8M1, Canada
PO Box 2090, Oroville, WA, 98844, USA
www.mokeham.com

Cover photograph by JvL

ISBN 978-0-9919981-0-4

Contents

On the front cover

During the Nazi occupation more than 250 people were executed on *the Waalsdorpervlakte*, a plain in the dunes just outside The Hague. Among the very first were fifteen members of Resistance group 'De Geuzen' and three organizers of the February Strike, 'the eighteen dead'. They were killed on March 13, 1941 and are remembered in a famous poem by author and resistance fighter, Jan Campert (see page 13).

After the war a simple monument was erected on the plain, consisting of four crosses and a low concrete wall, inscribed with the years of occupation, *'1940-1945'*, and the words: *'Many compatriots sacrificed their lives here for your freedom. Enter this space with fitting reverence.'* On May 4, Remembrance Day (the Eve of Liberation Day), a ceremony is held there for which the Dutch flag is formed against the wall with pine cones.

Introduction

Anne van Arragon Hutten

Many stories about the 1945 liberation of Holland focus on the joy, the warm welcome for Allied soldiers, the gratitude that lives on in survivors' hearts. These stories beg the question: what was Holland liberated from? In this series we have written about hunger and deprivation, loss of freedom, abuse and murder. Some of the worst atrocities were seen in concentration camps.

In this volume, Cor Feenstra tells about passing through five different camps, and about his liberation from Camp Wöbbelin by the 82nd Airborne Division. The camps' liberation has been fairly well documented over the years. I watched one video that included interviews with some of the first soldiers to enter the death camps. Decades after the fact, one old former soldier was unable at first to talk about it. He broke into tears and sobs, and even after he regained the power of speech he could not at times continue. This video also showed historic film footage of the camps themselves. No thinking human can view these scenes without tears: the piles of naked dead bodies, the inside of barracks where, among the corpses, one leg slowly moves. As one former soldier said, he would like any Holocaust denier to watch these scenes and then say it didn't happen.

Bad as Cor Feenstra's memories are, the total extent of Hitler's reign of horror was greater than even war historians have known. It is only recently that an effort has been made to create a complete list of the various ghettos, slave labour camps, prisoner of war camps, extermination camps, brothels where women were forced to service German military personnel, and so-called 'care centres' where pregnant women were forcibly given abortions or their babies killed at birth. The most infamous of the killing sites have become part of the public consciousness: Auschwitz, Dachau, Bergen-Belsen, and the Warsaw ghetto, but there were many more places where human rights were systematically extinguished.

In January 2013, researchers at the United States Holocaust Memorial Museum said there were 42,500 different sites, mostly in Germany but also spread across Poland, Russia and other occupied countries. In all these places, people were abused, starved, killed, severely beaten, and experimented on. Between fifteen and twenty million people died or were imprisoned at these locations.

The majority of Dutch citizens never entered one of the camps. Any overview of World War ll would list mass starvation, forced labour, killings, and complete violation of human rights. The very worst of these were seen in the camps.

Yet those who 'only' survived bombings, loss of freedom, hunger, and starvation have their own horror stories to tell. We received one letter from a woman whose husband had recently died. She and her husband had discussed sending in their war stories, but 'whenever I brought it up, he began to shake and cry terribly'. This man had, as a child, been in the centre of Rotterdam when it was bombed, experienced terrible misery during the rest of the war, and just could not expose his story to strangers.

The wild exuberance seen at the time of Liberation, with its dancing in the streets, its embrace (often literal) of Canadian soldiers, and its ignoring of the usual norms, can only begin to be understood when set against the preceding five years. In fact, even survivors can only understand in part. Who can truly comprehend such a level of sustained and categorical evil?

Holland was finally free. The cost had been horrendous in terms of deaths, malnutrition, and an almost complete destruction of the country's economy. It would take years to repair the physical damage, and housing shortages were a major reason for the large number of citizens who decide to leave for other lands. These immigrants have been the main source of information for these books. We thank you!

Historical background

The liberation of Europe began on D-Day, June 6, 1944, when Allied forces landed in Normandy on the coast of France. As we saw in volume 8 of our wartime series, it took them until September 9 to reach the Dutch border, as an advance party of the American 113th Cavalry Group crossed the border near Maastricht, Limburg. Three days later, the 30th Infantry Division entered Limburg. Inhabitants of Valkenburg hid in underground caves when the Allies came under attack from German artillery.

The first Dutch towns to be liberated were Noordbeek, Mesch, Eijsden, Breust, Epen, and Slenaken, while the first major city to be freed was Maastricht, during the night of September 13-14. Then came Operation Market Garden, when British, American, and Polish paratroopers were dropped in the Arnhem area with hopes of capturing the bridges over the Rhine River. This became the biggest Allied failure of the war, but progress was made elsewhere.

On September 17 the American 101st Airborne Division successfully landed in Brabant. Fierce resistance came from German artillery, but with help from the Dutch Resistance, Eindhoven was liberated on September 18, as Americans coming from the north and British from the south met in the centre of town.

The island of Walcheren, situated at the western end of the Scheldt river delta, was rife with German bunkers, machine guns, barbed wire obstacles and mine fields. Some areas had been flooded to further deter Allied progress by land, sea, or air. On October 2, residents were told to evacuate, and the following day 243 Allied planes bombed Walcheren's main dyke. Some 160 residents drowned, unable to get out fast enough. Dykes at Vlissingen and Veere were struck next, flooding almost the entire island. On November 1, Allied troops finally landed on Walcheren and defeated remaining German forces. Walcheren was liberated, but it was mostly under water. Zeeuws-Vlaanderen and Beveland were liberated by Canadian, Polish, and British troops. The liberation of the rest of Brabant began on October 20, with Canadian forces coming up from Belgium and British forces coming from the east. By the beginning of December, much of Holland's south had been liberated, although the northeast of Limburg was not freed until February 1945. As the various parts of southern Holland were liberated, the population celebrated with great exuberance. Some observers, their minds on relatives and friends in the occupied north, found this exuberance hard to take.

On March 28, the 1st Canadian Army arrived from Germany at Dinxperlo, gradually liberating the provinces of Overijssel, Drenthe, Groningen, and Friesland during April. By May 2, all German resistance there had collapsed. Holland's starving west, however, remained under German control when the Allies failed to overcome the heavy German resistance at the Grebbe Line. This was a forward defense line of the 'Dutch Water Line', a meandering diagonal line drawn through the country from north of the Dutch Rhine at Rhenen, where the Grebbeberg (Grebbe Mountain) was located, all the way to Holland's great inland sea, the Ijsselmeer. Begun in 1745, it was built on the principle of flooding low-lying areas to stop invading forces. It was first used in 1794, ultimately without success, against the French. The Grebbe Line was well maintained until late in the 1800s, and then fell into neglect. By 1926, whole sections had been removed.

When a German invasion appeared likely in 1939, the Grebbe Line was once again fortified. General Winkelman decided to mount his main defenses there in 1940, and flooding was initiated between the Grebbeberg and IJssel Lake. The German invaders, however, were held back for only a few days by the Dutch army, which was soon overwhelmed by the massively superior German forces. The worst of the fighting took place at the Grebbeberg.

During the war, the defenses along the Grebbe Line were largely removed, but in October 1944, the Germans decided to repair it for their own benefit as Allies approached from the south. Both Dutch and Russian forced labour was used, and in March of 1945 more than 12,000 people were building new forts and bunkers along the line. The Germans were determined to retain Holland, as it was an excellent place from which to launch V2 rockets at London. To slow down the Allies, they inundated much of Gelderland's Betuwe area and flooded the Wieringermeer Polder.

During April, the German army was still racing to prepare the Grebbe Line for battle. Fighting between Allies and Germans continued in various places, sometimes coming near the line. By April 24, discussions about the plight of starving citizens were initiated between the Allies and occupying forces. Seyss-Inquart, Reichskommissar of the occupied Dutch territory, had already indicated his willingness to halt further flooding if the Allies would not proceed past the Grebbe Line.

Instigated by US General Eisenhower, the conversation shifted to food drops for the starving cities. In effect, the Canadian forces halted their advance temporarily to save the civilian population of the cities. Food drops commenced on April 29. Road transports followed, with Canadian and British food trucks crossing the Grebbe Line.

On May 4, Field Marshall Montgomery accepted the surrender of German troops in northwest Europe, effective 8 a.m. on May 5. This should have been the end of the war, but General Blaskowitz, commander-in-chief of German forces in the still occupied part of the Netherlands refused to accept the validity of the German surrender on behalf of his troops. He was immediately summoned to 'Hotel de Wereld' in Wageningen to meet with Dutch and British officials, including the Dutch queen's son in law, Prince Bernhard, commander of the Dutch forces. On May 6, Blaskowitz belatedly signed the capitulation of all German forces in Holland. Apparently no typewriter could be found, causing the one-day delay. On May 8, the final and complete surrender of Germany took place in Berlin. Hitler had already been dead for eight days. Although the death penalty was abolished in The Netherlands in 1870, after Liberation the government reverted to a decision taken during World War ll, and reinstated the death penalty as an exceptional measure to deal with the worst of the war criminals. In total, thirty-nine war criminals were executed by firing squad, among them one woman. The last execution took place on March 21, 1952, the delay partly being due to the appeals process and the desire to be very sure of each person's guilt.

The records show that Dutch SS member Andries Pieters during the last weeks of the war had been guilty of inflicting the worst kind of torture, as well as actual killings, at a castle in Brummen, near Zutphen. Artur Albrecht, a German SS commander who headed the SD (Sicherheitsdienst) at Leeuwarden, was found guilty of similar atrocities. By the time these cases were tried, public support for capital punishment had begun to weaken, and the death penalty was not carried out again. However, in the immediate aftermath of the war, most Dutch people had understandably supported it.

Song of the eighteen dead

Jan Campert (1902-1943)
(translated by Anne van Arragon Hutten)

A cell is but two meters long,
Barely two meters wide,
But smaller yet the plot of land
Where I will soon abide,
Where, nameless, I'll soon take my rest,
With others take my leave.
We once were eighteen friends in here,
But none will see the eve.

O loveliness of light and land,
Of Holland's freedom coast,
Conquered by evil from without -
How could I only boast?
How can a man, honest and true
Sit still with such a blight?
I kissed my child, I kissed my wife,
And fought the losing fight.

I knew the risk when I began,
Aware that I could die;
A heart that can not bear the foe
Can not stand idly by.
I knew that freedom in this land
Was honoured in the deed
Until a damned and wrongful hand
Issued its evil creed.

A hand that violated oath,
Ignored its previous vow,
Invading Holland's lands at will,
Wanting to make us bow,
Pretending honour, but in fact
With fascistic belief
Turning our people into slaves,
And plundering like a thief.

That cursed Pied Piper of Berlin
Pipes now his melody.
As surely as I soon will die,
And ne'er my love will see,
And no more sit and share her bread
Or sleep once more with her,
Reject all that he offers you!
That whited sepulchre!

Remember, all who read these words,
My friends condemned to die,
And even more their loved ones
In their calamity.
For neighbours, friends, and family,
We fought the valiant fight.
One day the dawn once more will break,
And sun will follow night.

I see the first glimmer of light
Pierce windows barred with steel.
My God! please help me die today;
And if I sometimes failed,
As everyone can fail at times,
Still help, so that I can,
When faced with rifles to my chest,
Stand up, and die a man.

Flooding the Wieringermeer

Christina M. Sobole van der Kroon

On April 17, 1945, German forces blew up the dikes that had created the Wieringermeer Polder in 1930. Everything that had been built up in the previous fifteen years, primarily farms on the newly regained land, was inundated. The depth of the water ranged from two to fifteen feet across the entire area. The population had been given nine hours' warning to clear out.

The Hunger Winter continued to get worse. A loaf of bread was selling for thirty-five guilders on the black market. My sister Rie and I used to go to the Wieringermeer Polder to find food for the family. We had already made connections with several farmers, one of whom had the same last name as us but was not related. This farmer let us sleep in the stable the first time, and in the guest room the next. On these trips we used to exchange sugar and salt, which had been allotted to us because of our pickling business. But since the business did not function any more, we used it for trade.

When we made our last trip, we had nothing to trade any more except bottles of brine from barrels of pickled gherkins. The bikes we rode were heavy with makeshift tires made from old car tires, fastened with wires. The weight of the brine bottles added to the load.

I detested the Wieringermeer Polder. Almost 30,000 acres of desolate land, the first polder taken from the

Zuiderzee in 1930. The soil looked barren and white, stretching as far as the eye could see. The wind constantly howled from all directions, blowing up the sand with particles of fossils from the dried-up sea floor. Only the farmhouses, few and far between, provided shelter.

The distance between Amsterdam and the polder is about 50 miles. We stopped with relatives in Hoorn, about halfway, for a rest and a good meal. When we finally got to the polder it was unusually quiet. We saw before us a procession of horse-drawn carts loaded with cattle and furniture. We saw cats and dogs in trees, hanging on for dear life. We saw pigs swimming, trying to find dry land, and chickens trying to lift themselves out of the water. We kept looking at this vast specter; was it real, or a bad dream?

The water was slowly rising and it became clear that the farmers needed to expedite their transit out of the polder. We realized that we could do nothing to help them. We knelt down, unable to watch the scene any longer. If only we had had a camera to capture this scene. Very few people, except the farmers, witnessed this historic, tragic event.

Distraught and disappointed we headed home. By the time we got to Purmerend we had to push our bikes because of a bad snowstorm, which was unusual for the time of year. At the edge of Amsterdam, German soldiers looked through our luggage for food. All they found were bottles of brine, which we were allowed to keep. It is almost unimaginable that we did arrive home safely. Rie, however, got sick with asthma.

The Wieringermeer Polder was pumped dry again in 1946.

I simply can't forget

Gerry Bijwaard

By October 1944, the food ration amounted to 1400 calories; three months later it was down to 500 calories. The average city person lived on vegetables, tulip bulbs, sugar beets, and potato or cabbage soup from the Central Kitchen, which operated with the cooperation of the German forces. Dogs and cats mysteriously disappeared, and people slaughtered the graceful white swans that were swimming in the ponds. In utter desperation people stole from each other. Small garden plots were particular targets and had to be guarded.

Malnutrition started to take its toll, the weakened people falling prey to tuberculosis, dysentery, typhus, and diphtheria. Although my family was not as badly off as those in the big cities, I could see that my parents were getting thinner. My younger brother and I were often sick, especially when we ate something we were not used to anymore. My mother often went without food, telling us she would eat with our dad and telling my father she had eaten with us. One day we gathered at the table, but mother had nothing for us to eat. I have seen my father cry only once in my life; it was on that occasion. I remember feeling a great deal of bitterness and resentment towards those who had ultimately caused this. That same day I went to the German kitchen in the old barracks, broke in, and stole a couple of pounds of ground beef. I wrapped the meat in a scarf, and with great fear I ran to the nearest street corner, expecting to be shot in the back but nobody had noticed. The meat kept us going for some time.

The Swedish Red Cross, aware of the terrible conditions in Holland, sent a ship with food. I remember standing in line for hours wondering what we would receive. When it was my turn, a smiling nurse, whose face I will never forget, gave me a piece of white bread. I guarded the bread with my life and ran home to discover that it was badly molded. I did not care. I ate a thin slice every day for a week.

On April 26, 1945, the Allies started their food runs. The British called their project 'Operation Manna'; the Americans named theirs 'Chowhound'. This time the bombers were on a mission of mercy. The B17s and Lancasters came in low, their engines roaring in the quiet of the early morning. We could see that the doors were open, and when they came over a soccer field, the cargo was pushed out. The authorities immediately surrounded the many boxes and cartons that were scattered all over the field, fearing a riot. It did not happen. There was still some respect for law and order left in the hearts of the suffering people. The food was loaded on trucks and taken to a distribution point where it was fairly distributed among the hungry public. I got a can of Canadian bacon and some crackers. I did not dare eat the bacon, because I suffered from dysentery and my mother had told me it would make me sicker. The night of the food drop the Central Kitchen prepared its best meal of the war.

We were finally liberated on May 5th, 1945. It was high time, because all of us, including the Germans, were in bad shape. It took months before we could continue our lives in a normal way. I had to cope with dysentery until the end of the summer, often passing out. I developed jaundice also, but because of increasingly better nutrition, I slowly improved. Others were not so lucky and had to live with their problems for the rest of their lives.

One does not always have a chance to personally thank the people who provided help, but I had this chance much later in life, at the end of April 1990. On my way to Holland by way of London, while waiting to board a Pan-Am flight to Amsterdam, I noticed several older Americans, dressed in blue blazers. The emblem on their left pocket showed a bomber with the word 'Chowhound' underneath. With their wives they were on their way to Holland for a reunion and to participate in Holland's 45th year remembrance of Liberation. I walked up to them, gratefully shook their hands, and told them that I was one of many whose lives had been saved. At that moment, when I felt the emotion coming up in me, I decided to close the book on that whole miserable experience; that walking around with this for 45 years had been long enough. However, I have not been successful. I simply cannot forget.

My autograph album

Anthonia Huysman-Bamberg

I remember Mother bicycling to the countryside. In a few days, a truck would pull up and take out some of our mahogany furniture, and she would be able to buy vegetables and fruit, at least for a little while.

We remember May 1945 as a big party with food falling from the sky. I have some nice autographs in my poesie album, autograph album, all from Canadian soldiers. I'm always sorry I never tried to follow up to thank them.

Our eyes were big

Johanna Oostra

I was born in 1933. The first six years of my life we lived in Scheveningen on the North Sea, right next to The Hague. In 1940 my dad got a job as a milk truck driver. To be closer to his work we moved to The Hague. I was now seven, my brother four years old.

In September 1944 the schools closed, as there was no coal to heat them. Gas and electricity had been cut off and there were no candles. If we were lucky, Mom could bargain for a bit of oil for our lamp. That winter we lived mainly in our small kitchen.

Because of the rail strike no more supplies came in. We had nothing. Early in the mornings Mom and I would go to the nearby forest to steal wood. Just small sticks so she could use them in our potbellied stove for cooking and heating. My brother and I would go to the railroad tracks with a strainer and bucket every day, and search for coals amongst the stones.

By January we started to eat tulip bulbs. We cooked them, and also sugar beets. The beets needed to be peeled, sliced and cooked, and then you made pulp. If you still had a bit of flour you made a pancake. People were dying from hunger. Mom would pray and ask the Lord what to eat the next day. Sometimes there might be a knock on our door and a friend would share some wheat flour or dried peas.

One day in March we did get good news. The Red Cross was giving us one loaf of white bread per family. Mom sent me for it and I got the bread. The next ten minutes walking home were amazingly scary. I was halfway home when I knew that I needed to sit down or I would faint. I sat down on the edge of the sidewalk. A bit later I was able to go on. What a feast we had. My brother and I were sure this must be the taste of cake.

By April we looked really poor, eyes were big, no fat on the bones. To this day I remember it well. With the Lord's help we managed to hang on by eating the tulip bulbs and sugar beets, although they too were getting scarce and expensive. Our clothing too had become worn, and we kids had grown out of ours. Nothing new was available to buy.

Thankfully, on May 5 our city was liberated. American and Canadian planes flew over and parachuted five-gallon tins of food. They contained crackers, Crisco shortening, sugar and egg powder. It tasted so very good.

Angels of mercy

Petronella Vanderdonk

I was born in Culemborg, close to Utrecht, and was sixteen when the war began.

My father was a cigar maker, and I worked in a clothing workshop. We only had one slice of bread a day each, with ten children at home. I can still see my father slicing bread in the evenings, saying: "You can have your slice of bread tonight or you can have it for breakfast in the morning." Potatoes were scarce too. We had to save the potato peels, which Mom would boil the next day and mash with red cabbage or whatever was available.

I used to sew for people on a farm and when I went there they gave me a nice meal. But even these people had no meat, so there was no gravy. The lady used white sugar and browned it in a frying pan, then added a spoonful of lard, and water, and that was the gravy. When she gave me a piece of bread she would put lard on it instead of butter.

Towards the end of the war there were no potatoes any more. The Germans used them to shoot off their V2s. Two of my older brothers spent two years in German work camps, so it was my job to go to the Central Kitchen for soup. We often went to bed hungry. When those airplanes came over and dropped those big crates of food, oh my! I still remember those great big cans of bully beef, canned meat.

I very much remember the Canadian soldiers who liberated us, since I married one of them. They were our angels of mercy. I first saw two military policemen on motorbikes coming into town. They wore white cuffs and puttees. I still get emotional thinking about it. They were followed by military vehicles that distributed chocolate bars and candy. I got a whole chocolate bar and ate it all. Being the oldest in my family, I was tired of having to share everything. But that chocolate made me miserably sick. My stomach had shrunk too much after many months of not having enough food.

I met this Canadian soldier at a dance, Manny Amirault. My sister and I brought him home to my family, and they gave him surrogate tea made from tulip bulbs. He took off for his unit and came back with a tin of real tea, and other foods. Within two weeks Manny asked me to marry him, and my parents quickly gave their consent. I always said that they traded me for tea and coffee. I made Manny wait three months before I married him. He went back to Nova Scotia without me. In 1946 I was one of the first war brides to leave The Netherlands. I got priority because I was pregnant. When I arrived in Canada I was 5'8" and weighed 105 pounds. During the war, everybody was thin.

Editor's note: Firing off a V2 rocket used a good part of Holland's scarce food supplies. Kerosene made from coal had been used to fuel the V1, but for each V2, ten tonnes of potatoes had to be distilled to make methanol. The cost of each V2 exceeded that of a four-engine bomber, which would be far more useful and could be re-used indefinitely.

We pressed our bodies against the wall

Ann Mons Veldhuis

One week before Zutphen was liberated on April 8, we had gone to stay with my aunt in Beuker Street, as she had a house with a basement where we could find shelter. A lot of fighting was going on. I remember sitting in the basement and seeing the boots of a German soldier right in front of the basement window. We had to be very quiet so as not to draw attention to ourselves.

On April 8 we were liberated. People were ecstatic, and dancing in the streets. Prince Bernhard drove through the town in a jeep. Soon we were back in our own house again.

A week later, on a Sunday evening as we were sitting down to dinner, we heard the piercing sound of a grenade hitting the ground very close to our home. My grandfather looked at his hand, which was bleeding from a fragment that had gone through the window and the drapes into his hand. Then we heard another one hit nearby. My mother told my sister Fenny and me that if there was another one coming, to start running right after it exploded, and get to the shelter which was at least 300 yards from our house. So after the next one we ran, but were just halfway when my sister yelled: "Stand against the wall!" We'd barely pressed our bodies against the wall when a grenade exploded a few feet in front of us, spraying fragments into the wall around us. The miracle was that neither of us was hurt, not even by a small fragment. That night we stayed with an aunt and uncle. Later on we learned that not all the Germans had left after our liberation, but that some still lingered here and there.

Captain Hill

Johanna VandenBroek

Octeber 14, 1944 is etched in my memory forever. It seemed to me that the grass had never been greener; the sun had never shone brighter than on that Saturday morning. As I left on an errand for my mother, I felt glorious because we were free from the hated enemy that had been driven back five or seven miles from where we lived. At night, the enemy still came very close to our farm, but who cared, with hundreds of Allied soldiers to keep watch?

On my way back there was still the awesome sound of thundering cannons but I was not afraid any more. I saw a small military plane - the soldiers called it a 'Betsy' - circling around the house and then toward me. I threw what I was carrying high up into the air and waved with both arms. I saw that the pilot was waving back at me. Did my red sweater get his attention, or did he too, on this beautiful morning, feel a new zest for life?

When I returned home, my brother and sister were in the back yard. With the enthusiasm of a seventeen-year-old I told them about the pilot who had waved to me. As we talked, he circled again over our apple orchard as the cannons still thundered on. All of a sudden there was a ball of fire and the small plane came down in pieces behind the apple trees. Black puffs of smoke hung in the air.

What a shock! It was unbelievable; a terrible thing had just happened. Soldiers who had also seen it, explained that it had been one of their own projectiles that had hit the plane. Why? Had nobody warned them that this could happen?

I went inside, turned off by the indifference of the soldiers, while realizing how hard these young fellows had become in the war. My intense happiness gave way to a deep sadness.

Later there was a knock on the door and a minister asked if he could take some flowers from our garden to the grave of the pilot who had just been killed. He was to be buried at two o'clock. When we went to the funeral, we saw a neighbour carrying the dahlias, the only flowers left in our October garden.

We saw the stretcher carrying the body, wrapped in a grey blanket. I could see the soldiers' boots covered in mud. A grave had been dug in a neighbour's pasture. As the minister recited some prayers, we and about thirty soldiers looked on. Eight of them wore the uniform of the Royal Canadian Air Force. The Last Post sounded. As the last note died away there was complete silence. The cannons held their fire.

Then the minister put the first shovel of sand on the blanketed body. I could not help crying. Three short hours ago, so full of life; and now, lying in a shallow grave, no coffin, no relatives, not even a flag to honour him. To my surprise the minister came to me and asked me to put the next shovelful of soil on the dead soldier. My sister and brothers and all the soldiers did the same. When it was over we went home in silence. I looked back and saw the minister and a Red Cross soldier putting his name on a little white cross: Captain Hill. The planes were always dropping tin foil and later we made a wreath and a border chain from these. It seemed appropriate.

In the days and weeks that followed, my thoughts were often with the pilot's family. How I wished I could have told them the story of his death, and bring back his last farewell to all his loved ones for him. In July they moved his body to a military graveyard in Overloon, to be interred with his fallen comrades. When my girlfriend and I visited his new grave, sadness flowed over me again as we realized the soil in which he lay was so sandy that no grass or flowers would ever grow there. I wished he had been left in our neighbourhood where we could tend to his grave.

We emigrated to Canada, and returned for a visit twelve and a half years later. During this visit my brother took us to Captain Hill's grave, and I was surprised to see that it had been moved again, this time to a military cemetery with green grass and flowers. I was also surprised to discover, as I looked up his name in the memory book, that he had been only twenty-four, and not forty as I had always imagined. He had been married for only one year to Joan Mary Hill. Again I wished I could have told her the story of his death and funeral, but there was no address. Captain Hill must have been a very beloved human being. The inscription at the bottom of his memorial said it so well: "This rich dust, a richer dust concealed."

Since then I have visited Holland twice more, and each time I visited his grave and looked in the book beside the everlasting flame in the memory chapel for his name.

To Switzerland

Ben Wind

We lived in Dinxperlo: father, mother, and eight kids. On March 23, 1945 the troops that had stalled all winter started their final offensive with much artillery fire. When Dad came home that night he said: "we have to get out of here." We went to a farm three miles away, where my older sister worked. The farmer had no cows anymore and the stable was cleaned out. They spread clean straw on the cement floor and that's where we slept for the next week.

On Good Friday, March 30, the first light armoured vehicle carefully drove past the farm. The only soldier in it warned us to stay put. Much to the men's delight, he threw a handful of cigarettes toward us. It didn't take long before the first tanks came, followed by mile after mile of tanks. Many thanks to the Scottish brigade that liberated us! Our town suffered badly from the week of fighting. Not a house was left undamaged. Our house was gone; we had to temporarily live with another family. Upstairs, the back of that house was shot away too. Walking down the hall you could see the outdoors. Two weeks later the clergy from all the churches organized a public thanksgiving service, and all the people came to thank God for giving us peace and freedom. In the middle of all the ruins there was a big celebration. The red, white and blue flags came out, people wore orange clothing, and the lights came back on after years of darkness. In October I took a Red Cross train to Switzerland where I stayed for three months to recuperate. A young, newlywed couple took me in.

Liberation of a Frisian farm

Bill de Groot

On Wednesday, April 4, 1945, Germans in automobiles and on motorcycles raced over the highway to Heerenveen. We could hear the constant whine of the Mustangs, Spitfires and Typhoons that were shooting at the fleeing Germans. During milking-time, two Spitfires came down low over the farm, spewing machine gun fire at two German cars on the highway. One of the cars completely burned, while the other was found to contain stolen sugar, syrup and cookies.

At 3:30 a.m. on Sunday, April 5, a bomb exploded not far from the farm, and we saw a bright flare moving up into the sky. Most likely the target was German movement on the highway towards Heerenveen. Two days later we watched a bombardment by rocket-firing Hawker Typhoons, in the direction of Wolvega. Allied tanks, tanks and more tanks rolled past our farm, most of them still carrying evidence of thankful citizens in previously liberated villages and towns.

Our small country road by now was in a mess and some tanks barely made it through the mud. One of them got stuck, a 'camel' tank, without the turret and ammunition compartment, but full of communications equipment.

On April 12, we were spreading manure on the meadow when we spotted three small armored, machine-gun toting scout cars, with members of the Royal Canadian Dragoons, who had an image of a jumping deer on their black head covers. I waved at them with my pitchfork, which prompted a machine-gun to be swung in my direction and binoculars to be raised. We were being liberated after five years of brutal German occupation. What great joy!

In the evening more trucks, tanks and artillery passed by, and towards dark, were parked on various farmyards. The soldiers handed out Sweet Caporal cigarettes, Fry's hot chocolate, and Wrigley's Sweet Sixteen chewing gum. Eggs were exchanged for cigarettes, and the farmers were generous. The soldiers carried Dutch banknotes with the image of Queen Wilhelmina.

On April 14, the heavy flow of military equipment was continuous, then halted because of German resistance in the forests around Heerenveen. After dark, we could see tracer bullets racing over the landscape. Three half-tracks arrived to take positions on a farm next to ours. They carried 75 mm artillery-pieces and fired on the German positions for most of the day. The officer in charge talked to me about his family in Canada and showed me some pictures he had in his wallet. He gave me one of the still hot 75mm shells as a souvenir, which I still have. A little later surrendering German soldiers marched by guarded by Canadian soldiers and members of the Dutch Resistance.

On April 17, the people of Friesland were asked to collect food for the starving citizens in the West.

May 5th 1945: Victory!

This is what a local newspaper wrote: "Would there ever be in world history a week with so many historical facts as during the one we just experienced? The deaths of Mussolini, Hitler, Goebbels and Goering, the capture of Berlin, the total destruction of German resistance in the north of Italy, the capture of several Nazi criminals, getting food to starving West-Holland, the unconditional surrender of entire German armies in Germany, The Netherlands, Denmark near Magdeburg and Munich and finally the surrender of Germany to Allied forces in Europe, which brought the long desired peace." That was in the May 11 issue of the local paper.

No resistance against disease

Cornelia Gilbert

I was born December 24, 1939 in The Hague, so I only remember the last years of the war. The bombs came out of the airplanes and we had to flatten ourselves against the walls of the house. The sirens howled around us. Later we looked at the Bezuidenhout, a suburb of The Hague. Everything lay in ruins.

During the Hunger Winter I was given milk powder and a little soup. We were all terribly thin, and people dropped down dead in the streets. I always sat on my grandfather's knee. On my fifth birthday I got a book, 'Danny goes shopping', by Leonard Roggeveen, and quickly learned to read. It was my only gift.

I always had an earache, and later, tuberculosis, scarlet fever, and pneumonia. We had no resistance against disease at all, after all the malnutrition.

My grandfather sat crying on the garden bench when the food parcels were dropped and it was Liberation. Then we had a big party on the street, sack races, all kinds of music. I was finally allowed to look out the window again, which had not been permitted before, because the Germans might have shot at us.

After the war I had to go to a place in the south of Limburg for six weeks to fatten up. That didn't happen, though, because I vomited constantly, and I was homesick, especially for my grandfather. The people at this place made me go to sleep just as I was, dirty from vomiting, and said I was a bad girl. On the way back home they reproached me for not having gained weight. I was sickly until I was about ten years old.

We sang the national anthem

Christine Dodenbier

We lived in Ede, Gelderland, only twelve miles from the Grebbeberg where so much fighting went on in 1940. After making it to the southern part of Holland the Allies were unable to push past the Rhine River. The people in that area were ordered to evacuate. Ede was on the borderline, so we could stay in our home.

On April 17 we looked out into the street and saw no people, not even a dog. A few German soldiers passed by and we heard shooting, then silence again. We had no idea what was going on.

Around 2:30 p.m. my mother sent me to one of our neighbours to get water from their outdoor pump. When I came back with a bucket of water I noticed people out on the street, then more and more, and with that came a feeling of great excitement.

"The liberators are coming!" they shouted. I could not believe it. For years we had built up our hopes and expectations of freedom, but by now it was too much to believe.

I delivered the water and joined an excited crowd.

Not long afterwards a big Canadian tank came rolling around a bend in the street, with several others behind it. What a sight that was! The tank stopped right in front of our house. On the top, a small metal door opened and we could see the soldiers, who were waving at us. People threw flowers at them, and as we gathered around that great steel giant, still in the front line of battle, someone started singing the national anthem, 'Wilhelmus van Nassouwe', which had been strictly forbidden for five years.

I can still feel and relive the emotion of that moment. We had been liberated!

Liberated from hell on earth

Cor Feenstra

I was arrested just after the Allied invasion of France that was D-Day, and spent the last ten months of the war in five different concentration camps. I was in Amersfoort first. You got hit if you didn't take your cap off quickly enough, and the fleas were terrible, but I had more to eat there than at home, because the Red Cross lady, Mrs. Overeem, brought food. The commandant was not a bad man; he didn't hit us, but an SS-man, Kotälla, was a beast. He would go up to the prisoners, raise his knee and kick them in the groin.

The SS emptied the camp on November 10, 1944, putting 1400 men on a train to a camp in Hamburg that held about 35,000 prisoners. This was Neuengamme, and it was hell on earth. When we arrived at the camp I saw another prisoner who had come from Amersfoort earlier. He told me they would take everything we had brought, and if I had any food I should give it to him. I had a jar of marmalade in my suitcase and gave it to him. He was right. They made us strip naked and we got nothing back except camp clothing. He and I later shared the marmalade.

We were given two slices of bread and a bowl of potato soup each day. I didn't have a dish so they put it in my hat, a broad-brimmed felt one taken from a Jewish prisoner. On my second day there, we had to stand at attention for 24 hours because there was a prisoner missing. It was cold and a soft rain was coming down. Many people died and we had to stack them up, five lengthwise and five across until they were five layers high. The stacks of 25 made it easy for the SS to count.

The man who helped me most was a communist, Louis de Visser. If you could survive for four or five months you had a pretty good chance of making it through. This man arranged for me to go to a smaller satellite camp where conditions wouldn't be quite as bad as in the big camps.

On December 3, I was transported in a boxcar with about fifty prisoners to Lehrbach. Allied planes were strafing the tracks so we had to stop all the time. The camp was not too bad; we had only two or three dead every day. We had to take shot-down airplane parts, sort the good parts and rebuild the engine. The whole production was under the direction of Hitler's architect, Albert Speer, who was not an SS man. We had a German who was in uniform but he had to work, too. He had no gun, and he helped me stay alive. He hated Hitler and the SS just as we did. I will never forget his name: Paul Frank. He went through the motions of making the Heil Hitler salute in case someone was watching, but actually would say something else, a bit obscene. We had an SS radio to repair - I was an electrician - and Paul stood by the radio with a spark plug tester in his hand, so we could hear the BBC. Once he got caught by an SS man who found the radio tube was still hot. You could hang for that. Sometimes Paul brought a sandwich and gave me part of it.

By April 2, 1945, we had been hearing gunfire for days. That morning the SS kicked us out and drove 125 of us into a small Dutch railroad boxcar suited for four cows. If you lifted up one foot, you had to put it down quickly again or someone else's foot would be there. We were hemmed in like sardines. There was no water and no way to relieve ourselves. The smell was terrible. Just before dark the SS opened the door and we threw out four bodies that had been hanging between us. They gave us some water and let us relieve ourselves; then they locked the door again. The train had to stop regularly, as the Allied planes were doing a good job on the tracks and bridges. We did not get any food but when the train stopped again we were allowed to put the bodies of those who had died on the side of the track. We finally stopped for the last time on April 5. There were about eighty of us left of the 125. We all had to strip and our clothing had to go through the lice-disinfecting machine.

The camp where we had now arrived was badly overcrowded, and on April 14 we were loaded up again, sixty per boxcar this time. The following day we stopped near the Elbe River at Wittenberg. We heard later that the prisoners had pried open the door of the boxcar in front of us and tried to escape. Most were Russians and many of them were shot.

We arrive at the Wöbbelin concentration camp in Mecklenburg on April 16. A book was written about that much later: 'Ten weeks Concentration Camp Wöbbelin' by Carina Baganz. I have that book, and she sure got her facts right. There were no mattresses or bedding, no windows, and only one water pump, with polluted water. The Easter 1945 roll call showed about 5000 prisoners. We had hardly any clothing or food. The rumor was that the Red Cross had arrived with food for us but we got nothing. The SS were smoking English cigarettes; they had confiscated the Red Cross packages.

Most of the prisoners were Russians, and in the last few days when we got no food they cannibalized the dead bodies. That's in the book too.

On May 2 at 9:15 a.m. the 82nd Airborne Division under General James Gavin liberated us. Our liberators were talking about putting us all into quarantine. I had dysentery and was in bad shape, but wanted to go home. I took off with two other Dutchmen, one of them from Putten. I later heard that the other prisoners had been put into quarantine about an hour after we left.

Thanks to the men of the 82nd Airborne, I am still alive. With the help of American and English forces we were back in Holland by May 5. I weighed ninety pounds. By Christmas of 1945 I was back to normal at 190 pounds.

My birthday in the basement

Elsa Abma

My hometown of Velp was only three miles from the centre of Arnhem where the battle raged in September 1944. Fortunately we could stay in our homes but the memories of the Hunger Winter that followed are forever etched in my brain.

At the time, our family included my parents, my 7-year-old brother, me, and a Jewish lady we were hiding from the Germans. Food was very scarce. I still see our Jewish friend eating small bites with a tiny spoon so that her small portion would last longer. At fourteen, I was still growing, but my parents could not buy new clothing for me. I remember my mom sewing a coat for me out of an old pair of drapes.

In the early spring we became desperate for food. One day my dad and I took our bicycles and loaded the back of them with some of our best bed linen and two of my dolls. We crossed the river by rowboat and found a farm where we could exchange these items for grain, potatoes and vegetables, and a piece of bacon.

We fetched water in buckets from a pump outside the town. On April 1, 1945, the Allies launched an attack, and one of their small smoke bombs exploded on our storage shed, causing a small fire, which our neighbours extinguished. On April 2, my 15th birthday, it became too dangerous to stay at ground level and we took refuge in the basement, which was about 15 square feet.

After the war was over I read that during the night of April 14-15, 70,000 projectiles had been fired at my hometown in two hours' time. Finally, on the morning of April 16, there was total silence. We cautiously climbed the basement stairs and looked outside. At that moment the first Canadian foot soldiers came around the street corner. A German soldier climbed out of a manhole, raised his arms above his head, and surrendered without incident. Soon more Canadians wandered into our street, starting conversations and handing out crackers/ biscuits, cigarettes and white bread to all the hungry people who had gathered. Our Jewish friend also came outside after many months indoors, and mingled with the people. Thank God we were alive! The war was over. It seemed like a miracle had happened.

After our Canadian liberators moved on, American troops in jeeps followed. They provided us with powdered milk, powdered eggs, canned beans, corned beef, and white bread. It took months before our lives returned to some kind of normalcy. My widowed Jewish auntie was reunited with her two daughters, who had been in hiding elsewhere. When our mail was reinstated we received huge parcels from America, with basic food items and clothing. How grateful we were!

Restoring vehicles

Frans Dullemond

Finally, by the end of April, the British and Canadians liberated our town of Neede, it was cause for many celebrations and rounding up of NSB-members (collaborators) and Germans who had not managed to escape to Germany. They were marched off to Germany later. The house of the collaborating mayor was confiscated and given to a widow whose husband had been executed by the Germans because of underground activities. She had a little daughter about the age of my sister.

The English and Canadians were rather lax with their ammunition and we found cartridges everywhere. We soon found that we could easily remove the tips and then pour the black powder out. We made small trails of this stuff on the ground and then lit one end to see how quickly the fire got to the other end! Luckily we did not find any grenades.

Now the English were occupying the old railway station. Within the complex and all around town they had huge storage depots with thousands of jerry cans filled with gasoline. These were not difficult to open. Of course we played there as well. We got some gasoline in a tin and took it along to the station, where the Canadians had their cooking facilities. Against the wall we tried to light the gasoline. Well, it did burn, so much so that soon the flames towered above us. The Canadians were there in no time and had it out quickly. We learned very quickly not to play with that any more. It was at that spot where we got the occasional bar of chocolate. We found cigarettes everywhere, which of course we had to try. We got over that quickly too.

After the war, my dad got the task of restoring old vehicles, because transportation was needed more than ever, and new vehicles were not available. An Opel Olympia convertible had been hidden to prevent the Germans from taking it, but just after the war ended, the Internal Forces commandeered it for their use. Of course it came back badly damaged, as it had been rear-ended. My dad and his brother made a little van out of it and since they only had 2 mm thick sheet metal to work with, it closely resembled a tank.

One time Dad needed to go from Neede to Apeldoorn and he knew that a small freight train came by daily. He decided to hail the engineer and ask him for a ride. The engineer, driving a steam locomotive with one railcar, stopped. Dad asked for a ride and he was allowed on board under the condition that he would get off the train just before Winterswijk. Somewhere along their way the engineer stopped to collect some milk at a farm. Before Winterswijk dad got off the train and walked to the train station. There he could catch a steam train to Arnhem and in Arnhem a bus to Apeldoorn. The total distance covered was approximately seventy miles, while the normal distance is about half that.

The English troops became a source of food. My dad traded fresh potatoes for cans of food of any kind. The English apparently used lots of sheep for their meat, but they dumped scraps and bones. My dad collected those; my mother drew the fat from it all and canned it. For years we had a supply of mutton fat.

Life and death on Liberation Day

George Hansman

On May 5, the first Canadian troops entered Amsterdam, and many of us went to one of the bridges, to welcome them and try to jump on their vehicles to personally thank them. My friend with whom I spent most of the war did not come with me but decided instead to go Dam Square where many people were also expected to gather. Unfortunately, there was still a group of German marines in one of the hotels, and, seeing the crowd, they opened the windows of their first floor rooms and started shooting with machine guns.

When getting home that night I learned that my friend, trying to help a lady with a stroller get out of the line of fire, had been shot in the attempt and had died instantly. The next day his mother showed me a picture of his two sisters, a picture he always carried in his breast pocket. Three bullet holes had taken out their faces. Apparently the Germans capitulated after a short exchange of gunfire.

I will never forget the funeral. His body was temporarily placed in a church where the bodies of dozens of victims of starvation had been laid out in rows until burial arrangements could be made. Being one of the pallbearers, I had to enter the church. The smell was enough to take your breath away.

Several weeks after all the jubilation over liberation had died down, an action was held in Amsterdam to collect used clothing and furniture for the people of Arnhem, which had been badly bombed and damaged. The youth organization to which I belonged also helped out, and I teamed up with a pleasant girl working from the back of a truck. She had just returned with her girlfriend from a trip to a former concentration camp to find her brother who, with her father, had been picked up during an anti-resistance action the previous November. They had gone by bike to Amersfoort, and with help from Canadian soldiers they found him. They received a bike from camp guards and pushed him home, a distance of about thirty miles.

For many months afterwards we waited for her father, a former Amsterdam policeman, to return from a concentration camp in Germany, but, eventually, he was declared deceased. In 1949 the 'pleasant girl' became my wife.

No more getting up at night

Henny Merkley

On Friday, April 13, 1945 our neighbour came over to our house yelling that the 'Tommies' were coming; they were in Assen already. My Dad said, "I don't believe it; we will all die." All morning the Germans had been busy blowing up the airport and some bridges. We emerged from our bomb shelter to see some strange things: big tanks, healthy looking soldiers handing out cigarettes and chocolate, and we all waved and screamed, and then the shooting started. We ran back to our hiding hole while the tanks shot at the airport.

That night we saw our first Canadians across the road from our house. They came over with tea and crackers and we were so happy. The next day a new batch came to say the battle for Groningen had started. We saw the flames. They rounded up all the traitors in our village and put them on a wagon. Now they looked scared and cheap. For the young people like myself there were dances with Canadian soldiers at the school. They gave us chocolate and we had music.

After so much hardship and heartache we were all much older than our age. We grieved for the fellows who returned from Germany sick and old. It was a terrible five years. People being shot for nothing; the hunger; the ration coupons, nothing to buy anymore. We had food in our village but not the right kind. People got scabies, diphtheria, lice, you name it. But we had survived. No more blackouts, no more getting up at night, and no more Mam, Dad, my sister and I all in one bed so we could die together when the bombs fell.

It is no wonder that so many Dutch people emigrated to Canada, the USA, or Australia; they had had enough.

Georgian uprising on Texel

Klaas Korver

The island of Texel is my birthplace. In the spring of 1945, when I was eleven, we experienced a part of World War ll that few people are aware of. This was the Georgian Uprising, or the 'Russian War', as we called it.

At that time we were occupied by a battalion made up of about eight hundred Georgians and four hundred Germans. The Georgians were Red Army soldiers from the Georgian Soviet Socialist Republic, who had been captured on the Eastern front. These soldiers had been given the choice of remaining in prisoner of war camps, meaning almost certain death, or serving the Germans and be allowed some freedom. The battalion consisted of men who had chosen to join the Germans. They performed the same duties as the German soldiers.

In late March 1945, orders came to move several companies of this battalion to the Dutch mainland to oppose Allied advances. This was what triggered the rebellion. Shortly after midnight of April 5-6, the Georgians rose up and gained control of nearly the entire island. About four hundred German soldiers were killed in the initial uprising, almost all while sleeping. The Georgians used knives and bayonets. They were supported by members of the Dutch Resistance. However, they failed to secure the naval batteries on the southern and northern coasts of the island. The crews of these artillery installations were the only Germans still alive on the island.

The Germans ordered a counterattack and the intact batteries began firing at suspected rebel sites. This included a heavy bombardment of villages. We lived in open country on top of a dune, and I remember looking through binoculars, following the progress of this artillery bombardment and seeing the burning villages. Of course, this caused many civilian casualties.

German troops from the mainland were deployed and after two weeks of intermittent fighting, they retook Texel. No mercy was shown on either side. Captured Georgians were ordered to dig their own graves and remove their German uniforms before they were executed. My father witnessed part of such a drama. If civilians were discovered to be hiding Georgians, they were also executed and their houses were burned down.

The Germans kicked us out of our house and we became displaced persons for about a week. When we returned to the house it was of course a total mess inside, but at least it was not shelled as so many other houses were. I remember a German soldier telling my father that the Georgians were good marksmen, because in four days he had had four new commanders, each of whom had been picked off by the Georgians.

Out of about 800 Georgians, 228 survived. Till the end of the war, a few weeks after the Germans recaptured the island, these Georgians were either concealed by the people of the island, or they withdrew behind minefields where Germans did not dare go. At the time of writing two of these survivors, who are now about 90 years old, are still living in Georgia.

With the German capitulation on May 5 1945 World War ll ended formally for The Netherlands. However, that did not end the bloodshed on Texel. Officially, the Dutch Resistance fighters who were now 'above ground' were in charge, but the Germans and the Georgians held on to their weapons and kept fighting each other, causing more casualties. Finally, fifteen days after the capitulation, a small group of Canadians arrived on the island. They segregated the Germans and the Georgians, and disarmed them. Because of these prolonged skirmishes, Texel has sometimes been called Europe's last battlefield.

Texel had come relatively unscathed through five years of war, but for our small community this Russian War was a major disaster. 117 Civilians were killed, which, on a population of about 9000 people, was significant. About 565 Georgians and more than 800 Germans lost their lives. Many houses, and dozens of farms, were destroyed.

When people's backs are against the wall, they often do remarkable things; witness the fact that in a relatively short period of time much of the damage on the island was restored despite a severe lack of resources. I remind myself occasionally that we have far more abilities within us than we regularly use.

Memories of
the Liberation of Ommen

Enno Reckendorf

April 4 and 5, 1945: the Nieuwe Brug (New Bridge) was blown up again, this time by the Germans. Manitoba dragoons in tracked scout cars filled a small meadow while engineers constructed a Bailey bridge on pontoons, and off and on ramps, almost overnight. A burnt reconnaissance car sat in front of our house, and two dead NSB-men (uniformed collaborators) lay on the road in front of a nearby store. The next morning their bicycles were gone. Tanks tore up the northbound lane of the highway. The bridge in Ommen was blown up and repaired. Canadian troops were generous with chocolate and gum, traded cigarettes for fresh eggs.

Father came home!

Early May brought victory celebrations in Ommen's market place, with music, dancing, noise, and rifles shooting tracers into the sky. Some young women wore scarves to hide shaved heads: they had been sweethearts of German soldiers.

And then... back to lessons and books.

At a 1999 reunion of pre-war students, a monument honouring students who had not survived the Holocaust was dedicated on the grounds of the International School Eerde, with thirteen names carved in granite. Two names were those of my classmates.

Watching
the English army

Hans ten Bruggenkate

The liberation of The Netherlands took a lot of coordination between the various nationalities involved. I was fourteen, and living in Ruurlo in Gelderland's Achterhoek with my parents and sister. Our house had been requisitioned as office space for officers of the 10th Panzer Division of the Waffen SS. When they started firing their anti-aircraft guns, we fled to a farm just north of town. Our liberation came on April 1, with considerable fighting and a night spent in the basement.

The previous day, while chopping firewood in the shed, I looked out of a window and saw an armored vehicle racing up the farm's driveway, then back out again almost as quickly. It was a reconnaissance vehicle of the English army, complete with orange banners fastened to its front. That Sunday we saw an amazing display of military might in town. The Germans had fled to their Heimat, using stolen horses and wagons.

The English army, with numerous tanks and artillery, continued on to Borculo and Twente. We saw them firing at targets in Overijssel such as Rijssen and Nijverdal. It took several days for all the military vehicles to pass through, badly damaging the cobblestone streets with their tanks.

We had always expected our liberation to come from the direction of Arnhem, but it came from the enemy east. We knew that the Allies had finally managed to cross the Rhine at Remagen in Germany, and had heard heavy artillery one day.

This army we saw headed towards Hamburg. Soon afterwards came the Canadian forces, which attacked Zutphen. A tough battle lasting many days ensued. They built new Bailey bridges there to serve as routes into Germany.

All these happenings made an indelible impression on me.

Not a pretty sight

Hidde Yedema

The village of Makkum, Friesland, lies just south of the Barrier Dam (Afsluitdijk), that turned the Zuiderzee into a lake. Apart from a raid by the Gestapo one week before the liberation battle in April of 1945, when seven young men had been killed, the war had not meant much more than a shortage of fuel and clothing for us. For a child it was a bit of an adventurous time.

On April 15, the sidewalk across the street was full of soldiers. We were startled by a loud knock on the door. A soldier in his undershirt, and suspenders hanging down over his hips, stood there, saying, "Ich muss pissen" (I have to pee). We showed him the bathroom. When he came back to the front room where we stood open-mouthed, he started counting. "Eins, Zwei, Drei,"etc. Then he told Mem that he had eight kids himself and that he soon hoped to be back home with them again.

After Mass and breakfast I roamed the streets. Someone said the German Wehrmacht had left the airfield close to Leeuwarden and now wanted to defend the entrance to the Barrier Dam. The public school had been chosen as their headquarters. A kitchen wagon was moved into the schoolyard. The smell of food took me there, where I saw a young soldier, no older than seventeen, walking up and down the short street with a weapon over his shoulder. His hands were bandaged. He was singing softly, the only word I caught was Heimat, home.

His face was red, his eyelids swollen, and he had

to turn his head all the way to be able to see another soldier who was talking to him. I gathered that he was saying he wanted to go home. He needed help in taking a cigarette from its package and lighting it. When he said again that he wanted to go home, one soldier said, "Ssst, Willie! The Captain!" When a soldier with a high cap on his head came along, Willie was undaunted. He spoke to this man also, saying he just wanted to go home. That soldier took him to the kitchen wagon and let the cook load up two tins with food for them. They sat down against a wall and ate it. When they had finished, Willie started to sing and everyone joined in, singing the Heimat song.

The following Monday, the town crier announced that the area was going to be defended and violence was to be expected. A curfew would begin the following day, and everyone should find a safe place to stay, preferably below ground. All windows should be opened, or the air pressure of the expected blasts would break them.

Cellars were emptied, rain cisterns scooped out, earth shoveled against walls, and nerves were shattered. Food was packed in the hiding places, kids were told to get out of the way, then called back to stay close. My family decided to hole up in the back room, near the toilet. People with binoculars were on rooftops trying to find out what was happening. But another night went by with nothing happening. People defied the curfew, congregating in back yards.

Then, around noon, we heard a loud whistle, a louder scream, and a BANG. Everyone scrambled into their safe places. The bangs and whistles came without a pause, and glass was shattering. My younger sister and our two evacuees from Limburg cried their hearts out.

Mem led us in prayer. For us, it lasted an eternity. In reality, it was half an hour. Then... quiet.

We emerged in time to see soldiers in different uniforms, holding Willie by the elbow, bringing him to the end of the street where about twenty other German soldiers stood with their hands behind their head. I heard Willie talking to his escort, and heard the word, heimat. The soldier shook his head, emptying Willie's pockets, while Willie kept talking about his heimat. The soldier put back the handkerchief, threw away the pocketknife and the remainder of a pack of cigarettes. When Willie's tone of voice changed, the soldier looked at him. He then took cigarettes out of his own pocket, stuck one in Willie's mouth, and lit it. He stepped away, then changed his mind and put the cigarettes into Willie's breast pocket, along with the lighter. They marched away; Willie led by the arm by one of his comrades.

A grenade had come down in front of our house, damaging our furniture, and of course all the windows were gone in most of the village. I found out that Canadians had liberated us, and had to look at the atlas to find out where Canada was. These soldiers had not met with much resistance in Friesland, and only had to use force around Makkum and around Lemmer, both to the south of us.

A few days after May 5, a friend and I walked to the Barrier Dam, and I will never forget the sight we saw there. The remnants of the German army were being led back to Germany. A loose column of tired, bedraggled soldiers, limping and dragging themselves east. They were cold, hungry, and dejected, carrying only a mess kit and blanket. It was not a pretty sight.

My identification card was burned

Henry Niezen

The Dutch population was delirious with joy when the Canadians arrived to liberate them. We, in the city of Zwolle, were liberated by the French-Canadian Regiment de la Chaudière. At first it did not look very good. All the parks had been dug up and fortified with trenches. The Chaudières fired some rounds of artillery fire, whereby the daughter of family friends got killed. She was a young nurse, coming to the aid of a man who was lying in the street after having been hit by shrapnel. Another round killed her also. The Regiment de la Chaudière gave her a military funeral afterwards.

After the initial rounds of artillery, the Germans abandoned their positions on the night of April 7, and fled across the IJssel River bridge. They torched every building they had occupied. My confiscated photo identification card was burned in the Gestapo office. The liberation of Zwolle was completed on April 14, 1945.

What a relief on May 5, when the Germans finally surrendered.

The Germans knew they were losing the war

Jenny Blad

After liberation, a walk was organized from the farm we had been evacuated to, to our city, twelve miles away. The town was too burned for many to go back there. We had walked several miles when mother spotted army trucks coming our way. She walked to the middle of the road and held up her hands for them to stop. "Mama, you can't do that," I told her. But they stopped. The soldiers took the sick, the old and some of the children. When we had walked about six miles we came to a small village, Ten Boer. Some people stayed there, while my mother and my uncle got two bikes without tires, and with my sister and me on the back, we carried on to the city.

When we returned to Groningen, we stopped at my aunt's place. We found my grandmother there who told us that the Germans had killed her daughter, my aunt, who had spotted German army trucks unloading food at a school and she had taken some. The Germans had seen her, but had done nothing. Then she and a neighbour returned to get more food. This time the Germans shot in the air to warn them. My aunt did not believe that they would shoot her, and went on taking things. They shot her, killing her instantly. She left a husband and three boys. My mother's brother was killed also, but in a German prisoner of war camp. One of my nephews died of tuberculosis shortly after the war.

The Germans knew they were losing the war, but they did not want to admit it. My uncle did tell them and was promptly shot dead for his efforts. Not all the German soldiers were bad. It was the Nazis that were the real bad ones, not the common people; they too suffered. Many of the soldiers were just boys; they could be heard to say; "Ich habe der Krieg nicht gewillt." (I did not want the war).

In our street, a long table was set up with food, a feast. Later, if we told mother that we were hungry, she would get very upset. "I don't ever want you to use the word hunger again. You can have an appetite," she would tell us. Mother had risked her life many times; she had to give up her valuables for food, and the word hunger triggered something in her. People have told me that they had cooked and eaten poison ivy and that it tasted like spinach.

The Canadian soldiers, knowing we were walking behind them, would only take a few puffs on their cigarettes and toss the butts over their shoulder. I would give these to dad and he would roll them into new cigarettes.

Just because the war was over, did not mean that there was now plenty of food and goods to buy. Everything was rationed. Everywhere our city had suffered bombing and it took many years before all the scars were erased. For years we played in the trenches left behind by the Germans, and with the empty bullet shells. Slowly things went back to normal. I later had to help my dad with his milk route. His clients were mostly poor and I would always give them extra milk when dad was not looking.

My sister was a war bride

Jacoba Bessey

The highlight of the last phase of the war was the food drop in April of 1945. The Swedish Red Cross and the Royal Air Force got together and dropped thousands of pounds of food on the western part of Holland. Most of what they dropped was white bread and margarine. My brother, Hans, would ask Mom if the white bread was cake. It may not have been, but it sure tasted good.

Shortly after that the war was over, but it took a couple of weeks before supplies started to come in. The Allies, mostly Canadians, rolled into Haarlem with big tanks and handed out chocolate bars. The younger ones in our family had never tasted chocolate and were hesitant to eat it. The end of the war came as a great relief. It was nice to be able to spend time outdoors without the presence of the German troops and the Allied bombing raids.

My sister Johanna was eighteen at the end of the war, and we would ask her if she would date any of the Canadian soldiers. She said, "I never went out with a German, and I'm not going out with a Canadian."

Well, she did date a Canadian soldier and in 1946 she moved to Canada to join him. They celebrated their 50th wedding anniversary in 1995.

They gave us back our freedom

Joe Verstappen

During the first years after liberation everything was rationed. It took a while to get back to normal. We had learned how to do without, and lived accordingly. We learned to be frugal with the things that were available. I still have that in my bones, and can't waste food; I think that's a sin. We have learned a lot from the war years and it has helped our people to cope with hard times. Most of us immigrants have become prosperous and made a good life here in the USA and Canada. We learned to be careful. The war was a harsh teacher, and we feel blessed in the land of plenty. We are blessed by God in so many ways.

I wrote a number of poems as a tribute to the 101st Airborne Division, as I felt so full of gratitude for them giving us back our freedom. I was made an honorary member of the 101st Airborne Division, and of the West Coast Airborne Association. The old veterans would have tears in their eyes when I gave the poems to them. We owe them so much.

They retreated on their bicycles

John Keulen

In the fall and winter of 1944/45, the north of Holland, including Friesland, was still under German control. And so we had to wait in Friesland until the spring of 1945 before the Allies were able to push north. Father listened daily to the BBC broadcasts and had a good idea how far and how fast they were advancing. On the sixteenth of April he told us that the Canadian army was close, and that he expected them to liberate us the next day. He couldn't wait.

The Resistance distributed weapons and donned white armbands with the letters NBS (Netherlands Interior Forces) in big black letters. German troops started retreating on bicycles, as there was no fuel for their vehicles. The mighty Wehrmacht was reduced to a mere skeleton.

As dusk fell on April 16, the Resistance had what they thought was a brilliant idea. They would ambush the retreating Germans at a wooded location in Rijs by spanning the roadway with a rope that they would pull taut at the exact moment the German soldiers passed. In the resulting confusion of falling bicycles the NBS men would open fire from both sides of the road and kill as many Germans as possible.

After dark a large group of German soldiers approached on bicycles. All were armed to the teeth, not only with rifles and small arms, but also machine guns and hand grenades. In the face of this far superior force the NBS commander had second thoughts and whispered to his men to hold their fire. Their untrained ragtag band with Sten guns was no match for the well-trained professional German soldiers. The Germans never noticed the dozen or so men waiting in ambush, and continued their silent retreat eastward. The next day they were captured by the advancing Canadian army and made prisoners of war.

On the 17th of April, Canadian forces fanned out over all roads in the southwest corner of Friesland. Light armored vehicles entered Bakhuizen cheered by citizens waving Dutch flags that had been mothballed for five years. My father stopped the first Canadian Jeep and offered his services as an interpreter. They offered him a seat and sped off toward Stavoren. Father told them that the bulk of the Germans had left the day before but that they might encounter a few stragglers. He pointed out a large building that had just been vacated by the Germans as excellent headquarters for the Canadians. They moved in and established a field kitchen on the large front lawn.

My friend and I watched the Canadians do their daily chores. Father had taught me how to ask for chewing gum or chocolate in English, and they seemed to have plenty of both. My father organized an evening of dancing and music for the Canadians. Word was spread that girls were needed for the dance, and even some attached maidens wasted no time in getting spruced up for the evening. Although they couldn't understand each other, many of the girls fell in love with the young Canadians in their flashy uniforms. Romances blossomed and even resulted in some Dutch-Canadian babies being born nine months later. Their fathers left no trail, as usually only their first name was known. The story is as old as those of Hannibal and Genghis Khan.

The farm had no tap water

Nelia Barnfield

After liberation we used to go to the railway tracks to watch planes drop food parcels in the fields. I still have an addiction to crackers, which were distributed by the bagful.

There was a collaborator who lived around the corner from us, and he was arrested. They shaved his head, and put him on a handcart among the soap, towels, food and other things. Many grownups and kids followed this excitement. I watched from my second storey bedroom window.

I'm not sure when Winston Churchill visited Leiden, but I did see him in his open car, complete with cigar and Victory sign, not too far from the university. It was a very eventful time for a small child.

I was one of the lucky ones to be sent to a family in the countryside for a while. I believe it was our church that arranged those visits. They had no running water like we did in Leiden but they used collected rainwater which tasted rather bitter. This farm was near a large, very wide river, which was totally frozen over.

My mother's clivia plant

Nina Reitsma-de Groot

I remember the stories my parents told us about the liberation of Groningen. Two of my sisters and I were born during the Second World War. We were too young to remember much about the war and the occupation, but I remember the stories my parents told us later.

During the mobilization in May of 1940, my father was in the Dutch army. He was with the cavalry, since he was a veterinarian. He was responsible for the health care and safety of the horses. After the fighting was over and the Germans had taken over the country, he returned home.

We lived in a corner apartment on the ground floor of an apartment building. In front of our home was empty space; we were right on the edge of the city. In April of 1945 Allied troops finally made it to the outskirts of Groningen. Germans still occupied the city. For three days there was fighting. We were right in the middle of it. In front of us were Allied troops and behind us in the city were the Germans. Our upstairs neighbours spent those three days with us and the ten of us stayed in our small kitchen because that was the only room in the apartment that did not have windows, which meant it was the safest place. Every time the shooting stopped for a while someone would sneak out of the kitchen to check out the apartment and maybe quickly use the bathroom.

My mother said she was worried about her clivia plant

in the living room. She was very proud of it, because it had grown really tall with a flower in it. When someone left the kitchen and returned, they reported to her about that clivia. They would say: "Your clivia is all right but all the windows have bullet holes."

After three days the fighting stopped. None of us knew yet who had won, so when the door opened and soldiers stepped inside there was great relief when it turned out that they were Canadian. They were desperate for a drink of water. Then they gave us children some chocolate. We had never seen, let alone tasted, chocolate before. I tried a piece but thought it tasted awful and spat it right out. So the adults got to eat the chocolates.

It turned out that my mother's clivia had not survived after all. It looked all right from a distance, but up close you could see that a bullet had gone right through the stem. The plant still stood upright but that was because it was hanging in the ripped curtains.

It is no wonder that Canadians are so welcome in Holland. They fought, and liberated our country while many gave their life for our freedom.

Five days in the cellar

Lisette de Groot

As winter turned into spring, the Allies came closer and our town, Voorschoten, came under fire. By now the water was also shut off, as well as the gas and electricity. We decided it would be safer to sleep in the cellar. There were ten adults and three children, including my grandmothers, our evacuees, and us, with my brother in the cradle. My father assembled shelves from the apple racks on which to put mattresses. One of my grandmothers wanted to sleep upstairs, but my parents would not let her. This was a good thing because a grenade later damaged the bed on which she would have been sleeping. A big ceramic pot, normally used for sauerkraut, was used as a toilet and stood in a corner of the cellar. One older gentleman, an evacuee, refused to use it. Instead he went to the bathroom upstairs. He was quite deaf, so maybe he was not as disturbed by all the noise and danger as we were. When an Allied grenade hit the kitchen, there was much noise of an explosion, bricks falling, and the clattering of pans being knocked off the shelves.

One grenade landed in the septic tank next to the protected cellar window. Splash! It did not explode on impact. Finally, after five nights and four days, the Allies arrived in town.

My father had already pushed open the cellar door. This was not easy, because there was a five-inch layer of rubble on the kitchen floor. The roof was gone and he looked straight up into the blue sky. He also noticed that the aquarium on top of a cabinet was broken. All the water had run out. Dad realized then that the supposedly leaking water pipe had actually been the water running out of the aquarium. Nobody had remembered that we had been without water for days.

Although the bombing had stopped, we could hear tanks in the main street, and the rapid fire of machine guns. Gradually everyone went upstairs to assess the damage and listen to the sounds. I was too scared and refused to come out of the safety of the cellar. My parents let me be and walked to the main street to see what was going on. An hour later they came back, urging me to come up, as it was really safe. My nerves were shattered from the past few days, but I finally overcame my fear and we all went to see the 'Tommies', the soldiers in tanks handing out cigarettes and chocolate. The population was jubilant. Everyone suddenly had the Dutch red, white and blue flags waving in the wind and singing Oranje boven, referring to the Dutch House of Orange coming out on top.

It was an overwhelming feeling to be outside and free. The hated Germans were either killed or taken prisoner, and we were finally rid of them. Our family had survived, and that evening we slept in our own beds again.

My mother sat down and cried

Michael van der Boon

On the evening of May 4 we were sitting down to a meal of tulip bulbs and sugar beets, since that was all there was left, when we heard the rumbling of far-off explosions. I peeked through the planks that my grandfather had put in front of the windows and saw German soldiers unwinding what looked like cables.

My Dad told me the Germans were probably getting ready to blow up bridges. He had heard that the Allies were getting near. Needless to say, nobody slept that night. We sat around fully clothed, excitedly talking of things to come.

The following day is one I will never forget. It came with deafening explosions as the retreating Germans blew up bridges and buildings, just as my Dad had said. Slowly the sounds grew dimmer and farther away. We went through some hours of unforgettable pressure and fear, not knowing if the Germans were still around, and at the same time looking out for the first liberators. By noon an eerie silence had come over the city. Nobody moved and hardly a sound was heard. My father and grandfather finally couldn't stand it any longer and decided to have a look out in the street. I begged them to take me along, and my father, over my mother's objections, finally gave in. People were slowly coming out of their houses and from behind ruins and barricades. On a few balconies the Dutch flag was displayed, a gesture which took a lot of courage. I noticed it brought tears of joy to many eyes, including my Dad's and grandfather's.

At 6:00 p.m., two Canadian vehicles known as Bren gun carriers suddenly appeared. These very fast, small tanks came down the street to the welcoming roar of the crowd that had formed. But to our disappointment they turned around and left. Again it became quiet. People were still apprehensive because a few German soldiers could still be seen here and there; some on rooftops, making us believe they might be snipers.

By early evening people had become restless and impatient, and some returned home. Then, from the distance, came ever so faintly the chink-chink sound of tanks. We knew it was the time of deliverance. Mixed in with the sound of tanks, trucks, and jeeps we could hear a strange kind of music, which turned out to be Scottish Highlanders and their bagpipes. We couldn't believe our eyes and ears.

Members of the Resistance forces were still hunting down German snipers, but no one thought of danger as we rushed towards our liberators, yelling and crying. My Dad and I climbed on top of the tanks, hugging and kissing the soldiers. The huge tanks reached to the second floor of the houses, whirring and clanking down the narrow streets. Little khaki-coloured jeeps scurried in between the hundreds of large trucks and amphibious vehicles. Every car had the white star emblem of the invasion painted on top. Together they formed a dizzying stream of green and white.

People appeared from everywhere, unwashed and skinny, like rats crawling out of the ruins, falling into mortar holes full of rainwater in their haste to shake the hands of soldiers. The happiness was uncontrollable, with singing and dancing all around. I wanted to embrace everyone out of sheer ecstasy. To think that these Allies had come to free us! It was a fantastic display of power that eclipsed the German Army's drab, shabby uniforms, stolen bikes with wooden tires, and coal-fueled cars. Our whole family joined the throngs of people dancing hand in hand, singing the Dutch national anthem, hugging and carrying on throughout the night.

The soldiers, especially the Americans, handed out chocolate, chewing gum and cigarettes. it was the first time in my life that I tasted chocolate. They also handed out white bread. I brought home a chunk of bread with butter on it and gave it to my mother, who thanked me, sat down, and cried for a long time.

The Allied soldiers were clean and healthy. Not having seen healthy people in a long time, I kept staring at them. They seemed to me to be the real super-race, compared to that which Hitler had tried to create.

Most of my family was alive; we were the lucky ones. A week after liberation, my parents and I took an afternoon bicycle tour to where our house had been bombed. We saw that all the hedges were gone, used up for firewood. Flags were flying everywhere. Anybody who had enough strength left was on the street, repairing, cleaning, hauling away rubble, and rebuilding. German POWs had also been brought in to help clean up the mess. In the Bezuidenhout area, we stared at block upon block of ruins. Houses, church, train station - all was a mass of black rubble and twisted steel, with only an occasional building still standing.

Our house was totally gone. How lucky we were to have taken shelter during the bombing raids! We dug through the rubble and found some kitchen utensils, some of my dad's tools, and the stone head of my sister's doll. Dad packed it in a bag we had brought. We were utterly depressed as we rode on. Even though we had been prepared, it was still a great shock.

We saw a vindictive mob dragging a traitor from one of the houses and pushing him under a rolling tank. We saw several women with shaved heads and swastikas painted on their bare breasts being pushed around by the jeering crowd. We saw the Nazi prison where my Dad had been held for several weeks. Even with its horror fresh in our minds, its thick red walls seemed less formidable now. It had been given the moniker 'Orange Hotel' during the war, because resistance and patriots (loyal to the House of Orange) had been incarcerated there.

My father told us about one of his friends. The Red Cross people had found the whole family in bed: father, mother, and three children. The father had died on the day the Allies arrived but the others, too weak from malnutrition to move him, had kept the body in bed with them for several days.

Robby, the 18-year-old son of a former neighbour, who had just come out of a concentration camp, came over. He was Jewish and wanted to see if any of his Jewish neighbours might have survived. His parents had both been killed. As we were parting, Robby said, "Well, I am sure of one thing. I never want to see my children go to slaughter, like I saw my parents, I shall teach them to fight to the death."

Impetigo and lice

Pauline Hofman

On May 4, 1945, one of the boys next door came running down the street, waving his arms and shouting, "We are free! The war is over!" He tried to tell my mother that the Germans had capitulated to the Allied forces. I noticed a German soldier on a bike with no tires, in a shabby uniform but heading for the center of town. The neighbours came running into the street one by one while sharing the good news. Mom turned on the radio but no sound came out. After all these years of German-controlled programming, nothing! When Papa came home from The Hague that evening, he told us he had seen and heard the big news everywhere, even flags appearing in front of houses. People were still very cautious, with German soldiers still around.

The next morning, Canadian troops came past our house in their jeeps and other vehicles, handing out chocolate and cigarettes, and even letting some people ride with them. It was a glorious moment, and we tried touching the vehicles, even the Canadians inside them. Now we knew for sure it was peace. I was not allowed to take a ride into town with the Canadian soldiers, but my fifteen-year-old sister did.

The neighbourhood in no time flat organized a parade and other festivities, including a soccer match where the men had to wear creative costumes. My father, who had been the heavyweight boxing champion of the Netherlands, was dressed in his trunks and a white and blue bathrobe, and was skipping rope while playing in the game. I never laughed so hard as when Papa lost his robe and let the ball go because he was too busy skipping. My two friends and I were entered in the parade and were on the back of a truck, climbing a fence and jumping off while singing the nursery rhyme Drie kleine kleutertjes die zaten op een hek (Three tiny tots sat on a fence). We won third prize.

One day I had to go to the Resistance headquarters in the hotel where Papa was the chef. He had a small suitcase for me to carry home, filled with milk and eggs and even some coal for Mamma, who was pregnant with her seventh child. It was very heavy and I often had to stop for a rest.

When the girls who had dated German soldiers were having their heads shaved, I couldn't help thinking, "What if she had lice, like me?" My mother had sent me to the barbershop one day with a note telling the barber to shave my entire head, to get rid of the lice. However, I told him to just cut it shorter.

My younger sister had impetigo and had to have her head shaved. She also had to endure nightly scrubbing to get rid of the crusts, with new ointment applied afterwards. It took years to get rid of the lice. DDT powder, Lysol, and vinegar were tried to get rid of the critters, but no one knew that the bedding was probably full of nits. Eventually they did disappear.

We looked after Corrie

Nellie van Eyk

I grew up in Rotterdam. My sister and I trained in nursing at Zuidwal Hospital in The Hague before the war, and then traveled around to different countries, making many friends. One of our friends lived in Holland but when the war broke out he was called back to Germany to go in the army. We were very sad, and he said he didn't want to fight against his friends. Later we got a letter from his parents telling us that he had died in Russia.

One day, a little boy named Corrie who just needed tender loving care, was admitted to the hospital. He did not want to eat. His mama was out playing around with soldiers. His father was in a concentration camp. After a few weeks of nursing care, Corrie was okay but had no place to go. Children's Aid was unable to find a place for him, so my mother took him in and looked after him for four years. He grew up a happy little boy with wooden shoes, singing a lot.

After the Canadians liberated us, his father came out of the camp and took him home. That separation was hard for both families. I hope his life straightened out.

The farmers came out with shovels

Susan Rombeek

In the morning of April 13, 1945 many German cars and equipment drove on our road on their way to Groningen where there was going to be a big battle. We had tank moats dug around Noordlaren, and on the road were big contraptions filled with rocks to block the roads where the moats could not go. The Germans opened these and huge rocks fell all over the road as they passed through.

In Zuidlaren was a military hospital, and hours later I saw many wounded German soldiers, some on crutches, some with head wounds, walking all the way to Groningen, crawling over those rocks. It was a horrific sight, which I will never forget.

That afternoon the Canadians came. All the farmers came out with shovels and removed the rocks in minutes, so the Canadians could continue on to Groningen. Their command post was set up in the house of the school principal, where I had been staying. I now realized why people had never been very nice to my foster family; it turned out that the principal had supported the Germans. He was arrested and put in jail in Haren.

The principal's wife and daughter were given one room in the house, and I slept on a couch. The Canadians were not very nice to us, but when I explained that I came from The Hague and that my father was in the Resistance, things got a lot better for me.

There I stood
in my underwear, waving

Robert Colyn

Editor's note: Robert Colyn spent the war in The Netherlands while his parents were in the Dutch East Indies. Tiek Heinsius is the girl he would later marry.

By April, 1945, starvation in western Holland had reached such a catastrophic level that it could no longer be ignored by the Allied High Command in London. The staff of General Eisenhower initiated discussions with the German High Command in Holland, negotiating ways to drop food parcels at various airports near Amsterdam, Utrecht, The Hague, and Rotterdam. Starting on April 29, aerial food drops (Operation Manna) began.

While staying in hiding on a farm near Schiphol airport I saw the first wave of mercy flights coming right over me at low altitudes, enabling me to wave to crewmembers. It's hard to describe my emotions as I stood there in the open field, taking off my blue overalls and using them as a flag to wave with. No event in my life has stirred more intensely emotional feelings in me than the view of these liberators returning my greetings to them. Waving back to me, cargo doors open, they were ready to drop their lifesaving cargo. There I stood in my underwear, waving my blue garment, chilled to the bone because of icy winds buffeting me.

The liberation of Holland by the 2nd British Army,

which included a large contingent of Canadian and Polish soldiers and a brigade of Dutch soldiers, was celebrated by the population to such a high degree of jubilation as was never seen before in Dutch history. The festivities lasted for weeks. Every neighbourhood organized dances where we could enjoy Glenn Miller's and Tommy Dorsey's big-band swing music, swirling around on the city's streets and plazas, as long as our feet would endure it.

Fraternization with our liberators was at a very high peak. Soon it became evident that many Dutch women were smitten by these foreign heroes and started carrying their babies. One editorial in Amsterdam's largest newspaper, De Telegraaf, pointed out that in the next European war our future liberators would already be on our soil, since Canadian, British, and Polish offspring brought forth in The Netherlands after the war would be of age to be drafted for the defense of the country.

Tiek also met a dashing officer of the South-African contingent in the British army. She limited her fraternization with him to accepting his Players and Chesterfield cigarettes, along with some nylon stockings, and occasionally accepting his invitations to go jitterbugging at a nearby officers' club. By the time our new school year started in September, the country had settled in for a long and costly recuperation from the previous five years of death and destruction.

After the war in the Pacific ended in August 1945, a large portion of the Dutch in the Dutch East Indies were repatriated to the Netherlands. They included my parents and younger sister, Elizabeth. With the Netherlands already in a dire financial straitjacket due to the war years, it now had to face the costly burden of repatriating many tens of thousands of men and women. After their arrival in Holland, these emaciated survivors of prison camps and labour camps needed housing, medical care, schooling, and jobs. It was a monumental task for such a devastated country.

Eating paper

Rita Dijkstra

At the age of about three I remember sitting on a bare wooden floor eating paper during the Hunger Winter.

Another thing I remember is that it was very slippery in our street and when I ran outside, I promptly fell flat on my face. I looked up and came face to face with an enormous soldier wearing his gas mask, which scared the heck out of me since I had never seen one of those things. So on hands and knees I scrambled back inside.

After the war was over, many houses in the city of Utrecht were decorated with coloured balloons, banners, flowers, and large 'welcome home' sign with a lot of little orange paper flags. And we often heard 'Oranje boven!', referring to the House of Orange.

A couple of doors down from us lived a girl my age and we used to walk to school together. But one time my dad saw us, and boy did he get angry with me. He said if he ever saw me with that 'mof' (Kraut) again he would break both my legs. As I am part Jewish you can understand his anger. But at my age I had no idea what that word meant and was too scared to ask him. When I asked my friend about it she told me that her dad was German. Shortly thereafter they moved away.

My Canadian soldier

Ankie Bruigom

Among my family photos is a picture of my 'unknown soldier'. During Liberation festivities I bought this photo at our local photography shop, and held it for days on end. He was one of the many who gave us freedom after the terrible war. Over many moves this photo came with me. When I look at it I see myself, a ten-year-old girl, dancing in the streets. I wore a long nightie made of flowered fabric, and wore a red beret on my head. Grownups and children danced arm in arm in long rows, often singing the then popular Hokey-Pokey.

In April 2005, a local paper, in connection with a 60th anniversary celebration of Liberation, published information about the liberators, including my photo. I was invited to the Royal Canadian Legion for the ceremony and lunch. An hour before I left home I received a phone call from Campbell River, and a woman's voice said, "Your unknown soldier is unknown no longer." She had seen the photo in the paper. It was her brother, and she wanted to meet me during the ceremony. I told her she could recognize me by my walker. However, there were lots of old people with walkers, so it was no use.

After the ceremony we went to the Legion for lunch, where I was told "there's a lady here trying to find 'Ankie'. That was me. What a rare meeting that was! She had brought a box full of old photos. Her brother, she said, had died of cancer in 1995. She showed me pictures of his whole family; he had lived in Prince George. She was happy to hear that I had his photo on display with my family pictures.

From war to war

William Rooyakkers

Editor's note: For many young Dutchmen, the war was barely over when they were drafted for the war in the Dutch East Indies.

I spent time in a forced-labour camp in Germany, close to Munich. I escaped on October 10, 1943, and made it back to Holland three weeks later. I joined the Resistance, and in 1944 went into the province of Gelderland with the Internal Forces (part of the Resistance). We were in Wamel and Dreumel, both on the shores of the Waal River. Later, I was with the Canadians as they pushed into Germany. We went to Kleve and from there via Emmerich back into the Achterhoek as far as Zutphen. We had to keep moving, went back into Germany, and stayed there till the capitulation.

After that it was back to the barracks at Camp Vught. Later we were taken across to England for a short period of training. We left England from Southampton on the troop transport ship Alcantara, known as the 'Hunger Ship', for Indonesia. When we had almost arrived there after six weeks, British Lord Mountbatten ordered us to Batavia (Jakarta).

In February 1946 we were the first Dutch soldiers to land on the island of Banka. Later went to Batavia, and then to Palembang, in Sumatra. We were involved in the first police action there. In April 1948, the S.S. Zuiderkruis took us back to Holland.

At that time I left the army and became a bus driver until the Korean War broke out. I signed up again as a volunteer and went with the first batch of reinforcements to Korea, where I was wounded.

Who was that liberator?

Piet Vermeulen

Editor's note: On September 16, 1944, a squadron of Lancasters attacked the Moerdijk Bridge over the Hollands Diep river, between the north of Holland and the south. During the attack two planes crashed and fourteen lives were lost. One of the planes came down in a flooded area, and the Germans did not permit anyone to get near it. The other crashed just outside the town of Strijen. The crew, one of whom was Arnold Ney Johnston, was buried locally. Piet Vermeulen found out more about him long after emigrating to Canada.

Totally by coincidence I found out that Arnold Johnston was from the Blackstock area, near Bowmanville, Ontario, when I noticed his name on the local cenotaph. I was born and raised in Strijen, where he had died and I wanted to know more about him.

Someone put me in touch with Delton Dorrell, a cousin of Arnold's, who told me that Arnold had been born in 1916 on his parents' farm, the second of four children. The farm lies three miles east of Blackstock. The family kept a few cows, pigs, and chickens, growing their own hay and grain. During the 1920s times were good, but the 1930s brought hard times. Arnold used to take the family pick-up truck to sell produce to cottagers on Lake Scugog, raising much needed cash. Later he got a job with Canadian Tire in Toronto.

When WW ll broke out, Arnold and four school friends

signed up as volunteers for the RCAF, training in western Canada before leaving for England in 1942. Arnold told his family, "I believe it's a just war to liberate Europe. At the same time I look forward to adventure, but I'm afraid something will go wrong."

As a navigator, Arnold flew many times to Europe. His plane was the LM 693 of the 115th Squadron. Based on the record of his crewmate, Douglas Dawson, Arnold probably flew more than 25 missions during June-September 1944, many of them to France after D-Day, and to Stuttgart and Stettin in Germany. We don't know how many flights he had made in the three years before that. After he died, his father became very quiet while his mother suffered from depression for the rest of her life. Only one of Arnold's four friends survived the war.

When I stood at the cenotaph in Blackstock with Arnold's name on it, I asked myself, "Did he have to lose his life in my place of birth to give me the opportunity to emigrate as a 19-year-old boy to take his place in this big and beautiful country?"

Canned milk

Katherina de Leeuw

I was born and raised in The Hague. In December 1944, Dad was able to get our family on a truck going to Zwolle, in Overijssel. It took three days, mostly driving at night. We stayed in Zwolle with two old ladies. They had dried apples in the attic and we ate lots. Then we were taken to Friesland, to Rottevalle. My mother was unbalanced and ran away to Leeuwarden. My father was already sick with hunger oedema. But we had food and shelter. I could go to school. My brother worked on a farm. In May we went back to The Hague. There were no dogs or cats to be seen and lots of trees were gone.

Food came down from the sky. I do remember getting my hands on a can of sweetened milk, rich and thick. I ate it all and was sick as a dog, of course. Food was still very scarce after the war, and rationed.

Liberation of Gorinchem

Kees Vermeer

On the evening of May 4, around 8 p.m., I heard that the Germans had surrendered. I was 14 at the time and lived with my family on the outskirts of Gorinchem, next to a small park. Germans who operated a field hospital nearby had disappeared from our neighbourhood a few weeks earlier. The German 'Green Police' who occupied several houses on our street were gone too. That evening, a door across the street burst open and a neighbour appeared singing the Dutch national anthem. The Germans had surrendered. Everybody came out of their houses. Our feelings were indescribable!

A friend and I dragged a flare to the park. It had been dropped by the Allies but had not exploded. We pulled straw from the roof of a little shed that housed beehives, and placed the flare on top. We lit a match to the edge of the straw pile and ran like crazy. There was an explosion, flames and an unbelievably bright light that lit up the evening sky. Our neighbours ran to the edge of the park and cheered. I later heard that people three miles away had seen the bright light.

Germans had seen it too, but since the light had lasted only ten minutes they knew only its approximate location. As darkness fell, people returned to their homes. When German soldiers arrived on bicycles twenty minutes later, shouting and shooting, our street was empty. We continued to celebrate inside our house.

The next morning, a vehicle stopped in front of our

house. In the Jeep were two men dressed in khaki uniforms. They had chubby cheeks, unlike German soldiers who generally had taut faces. One of them had a cigarette dangling from his lower lip. The other had a gun in his hand, with a funny long spike at the end. I opened the door and said hello. When they responded in funny Dutch, I looked at them in amazement. I had expected Canadians, but they told me they were Belgians from Flanders. They asked me for directions, which I supplied, and off they went. That was my first introduction to the Allied forces.

Half an hour later I followed the Jeep's direction. Soon I came upon an amazing sight. Hundreds, or perhaps thousands of German soldiers were lined up in a long column that filled the entire street from beginning to end and beyond. They had come to a halt and stood there, some with a bicycle. None carried weapons. They looked completely dispirited, exhausted and defeated. This was what was left of the mighty German army.

A handful of Canadian soldiers headed the column. It looked as though they were guarding cattle going to the slaughterhouse. This handful of armed soldiers kept the entire giant German millipede at bay. Someone drew the attention of the Canadians to the bicycles some of the Germans were holding. The Canadians gestured to the Germans to drop them to the side of the street. The Dutch swarmed the bikes; it looked like a feeding frenzy. Many Dutch had a bicycle again.

In Hoornaar, five days later, I saw many Canadians armed to the teeth with automatic Sten and Bren guns guarding a field camp with German prisoners of war. The prisoners were being processed one by one, while armed Canadian soldiers were lying on roofs and on the ground, ready to fire. To me it looked a bit overdone. These were likely the same prisoners I had seen previously.

Canadians, mostly from Québec, took over the former German field hospital near our home. They often gave us a ride in their armed carriers. Many Dutch women were now dating the Canadian soldiers, including one girl who had previously dated German soldiers. Switching quickly to a Canadian may have saved her from the fate of other Dutch women who had dated Germans.

We boys traded in military commodities, chocolate bars, and Players cigarettes. With a friend, I even put together a German machine gun from parts disposed of by a German soldier. We had no fear of weapons and treated bullets as collectors' items. I obtained a flare pistol with cartridges that became an instant sensation. In the evening I would shoot flares in many different colours towards the sky. Even though my shoulder hurt from the kickback I kept firing the pistol as the thrill outweighed the pain.

I met my husband in Breda

Hetty Wear

At liberation time, people cut down the yellow and black road signs the Germans had put up. The first liberators we saw were British Royal Engineers: a lieutenant and about seven other men all billeted in our street. A neighbour who had a big kitchen got the cook, and they ate their meals there. The lieutenant asked my mother what was most needed, It was hard to answer. What was not needed? We needed flour, meat, butter, potatoes, everything.

In July 1945, I was at last able to visit my grandparents who were living in Breda. We had not been able to visit since the previous fall, as we lived in Gorinchem on the wrong side of the line. Now we cycled to Breda to spend two weeks there. At the start of our second week we met a Canadian officer as he came out of a neighbour's house .He asked if we would like tickets to a Saturday dance at the barracks. When he mentioned coffee and sandwiches afterwards, we decided to go. We went for the food.

A soldier came up and asked me to dance. This is how I met my future husband. Mostly he came to Corinchem but some weekends I would cycle to Breda. On October 31 we got engaged, John having ordered rings from Canada. When he found out that he would be shipped back to Canada in January, we quickly planned a wedding in December, and my wedding dress came from Canada. I arrived in Canada in June 1946, and

John traveled to Winnipeg to meet me. How wonderful it was to be able to do some shopping and look for some new clothes. After three days we boarded the train for Edmonton.

How we got home after the war

Frank VanderKley

I n May 1945 the Dutch were liberated and Canadian troops took over. The Germans were finished and everyone heaved a sigh of relief. I had just celebrated my birthday, with no presents, and was anxious to get back to The Hague where my family lived. My Dad came from somewhere on his bike and as before, my brother Frits sat on the luggage carrier in front of the handlebars and I sat on the rear luggage carrier. Frits was eight and I was eleven, so the combined weight was considerable. Dad would have to pedal about seventy miles to get us home. However, after about forty miles he was exhausted. At the side of the road two young women were talking to two Canadian soldiers. They had some kind of luxury car that was painted war green. I think it was a Citroën.

My Dad talked to the soldiers and somehow persuaded them to take us kids to The Hague. He would follow on the bike. It was decided that Frits could get on top of the luggage in the back seat, and I was to ride behind the spare tire which was fastened to the back of the car. I was wedged in, and in a rather dangerous position, facing the road. They told me to hit the car roof if the ride was too fast or too bouncy. If the bouncing had been really bad, I would have been mush on the pavement.

I have never been so scared in my life. I was hanging onto the tire with one hand and pounding the car roof with my other hand, but the speed never changed. Finally the ride came to an end and they let us out at the very north end of the city. I was completely lost, as I had never been there before. I had been told never to talk to strangers so we muddled on. I decided to follow the sun. I reasoned that we lived in the west end of the city and it was already afternoon. We walked for many miles when I suddenly saw a familiar landmark: the 300 foot high church tower in the centre of the city. From there I knew how to get to an uncle and some of my mother's aunts. Frits cried that his feet were sore and that he was tired. I grabbed his hand and dragged him along. We made it to Piet Hein Street, where our relatives were surprised to see us. I was happy that we were safe.

Ruins

Dirk Hoogeveen

On April 29 the first food drops took place. It was a tremendous sight to see those castles of the sky with wide-open doors flying low approaching the target site for unloading. However, it was another week before the food was actually distributed.

On May 5 long awaited freedom was ours. On May 8 we watched the mighty Canadian Army enter The Hague from an overpass. It lasted from eight in the morning until we went home that evening at about 8:00 p.m. and they still kept coming. After that came the removal of the German occupation forces.

When Queen Wilhelmina came to The Hague for the first time a few days later, we again chose that same spot on the highway. We had expected that she would simply drive by and maybe wave, but to our astonishment she had the car stopped, and greeted us within a handshake's distance

The months after the war were filled with honour parades of the Canadian Army in The Hague, the viewing of fleets from many Allied countries in Rotterdam with fireworks from the English warships, the triumphant return of the New Amsterdam, the many freedom festivities, et cetera.

It was also a period when we had to face reality. For many people return to 'normal' life never came. Men who came back from Germany sometimes found nothing to return to, or they found a totally changed family situation. The aftermath of the war lasted for many years. In December 1990, I read an article in Discover magazine about 'War Babies'. It described what happens when an expectant mother suffers from malnutrition. The study concluded that three generations later the grandchildren of the 40,000 women who were pregnant in the Hunger Winter, had a smaller birth weight, do not have good health, and have less resistance to disease.

Due to insufficient nutrition such as, for instance, not having enough iodine, the children of that time often have a thyroid problem, which, again, affects the next generation, as do some other illnesses.

I do not know whether Germany ever compensated The Netherlands for the damage of war. After the war the damage was estimated at 25 billion guilders, or four thousand guilders per inhabitant. The Dutch cattle herd was reduced by almost 30% and pigs by 70%. Only 10% of the poultry was left.

Approximately 100,000 hectares of agricultural land was flooded (8.5%), and, because of the manure shortage, agriculture yields would be 30% less than normal.

The whole infrastructure of the country lay in ruins. There was nothing much left of the railway system, for instance. Not only had many railway lines and the electrical overhead wires disappeared, but of the 890 locomotives only 165 were left, and of the 30,000 freight cars, only 1050 could be found. Of the 1750 passenger carriages there were 284 left. The 300 electric train-units were reduced to five, and of the 57 diesel electric train-units, only one was left. One can conclude that the Netherlands had gone bankrupt.

Tending the war cemeteries

Else Bevelander

My husband and I were both teenagers during the war, and it made a lifelong impact on us. We came to Canada in 1958, by plane, and have built up a good life here.

What influenced our decision to emigrate to Canada was the fact that it was the Canadians who liberated us. They were volunteers, young men, who suffered great losses. When visiting The Netherlands we went to their graves in cemeteries such as Groesbeek and de Holterberg. School children care for the graves and put fresh flowers on them. Where else in the world can you find that?

Afterword

Tom Bijvoet, publisher

At the close of this ninth and final book in our 'Dutch in Wartime' series, it is time to reflect briefly on the 'Dutch in Wartime' project. It started in 2009, in the run-up to the 65th anniversary of the liberation of The Netherlands in May of 2010, and concludes more than three years later with the memories of the final days of war and occupation, and of the exhilaration of liberation.

The project was initiated by some of the participants themselves. They started sending us their stories and urged us to publish them. As we received these, sometimes short, sometimes longer, memories of the war in The Netherlands, I was reminded of my youth. Growing up in 1960s Holland, the war still seemed to be everywhere and it appeared to be foremost on the mind of adults. Movies we saw were about the war; children's books we read were about the war; and stories our grandparents, parents and teachers told us were about the war. The adults in our lives had all experienced the Nazi occupation of The Netherlands either as young adults or as children, and we kept hearing the same stories over and over. It is in this repetition that their power lay – one story, two stories, three stories one can dismiss as anomalies, exceptions, but dozens of similar stories told by people from all walks of life emphasize the universality of the experience. And that is important because these were not just stories, these were lessons drawn from real life. Lessons about the devastating cruelty of war. About hardship, fear and pain, but also about camaraderie, compassion and courage. The civilian populations of countries at war are sucked into misery, however determined they are to continue life as usual. Trying to keep your head down and making do is an instinctive reaction. But external circumstances prevent just that.

These books are largely about the experiences of people with whom you can immediately identify. Stories about which you may think: 'how did you manage to cope with that for five long years – how did you even survive?' And, as we discover while we read about experience after experience, it took a large degree of everyday heroism simply to take care of your family and to continue living.

Some people may wonder occasionally why throngs of people, even those too young to have experienced the war, will turn out to cheer the last remaining veterans who parade down the streets of towns and villages once every five years when the people of the Netherlands celebrate their liberation from Nazi occupation. I am convinced that the stories in this series give ample clarification. I am the only contributor to 'The Dutch in Wartime' who has no firsthand experience of the war and I can safely say, after having read the stories of two hundred people who do, that I consider myself very fortunate for that, very fortunate indeed.

I am very thankful to all those people who mailed in their stories. For many it has taken courage to return in mind to those awful years. 'I always wanted to write this down for my kids and now I have a purpose,' I heard from several people. Others had already started that endeavour and sent me their drafts, or completed manuscripts. I am particularly grateful for the trust these two hundred people have given me in allowing me to publish their material. I hope I have not betrayed that trust.

Special thanks to Anne van Arragon Hutten who stepped in after three volumes to take over the editing of the books, a task that, with my other responsibilities, was beginning to overwhelm me. Any errors are my responsibility.

Without the encouragement of my wife Petra and my children Edina, Nicola, Ronesca and Piers, who saw me skip many a family activity to work on this book series, it would not exist. And as we are expressing our gratitude, anyone who reads this publication will join me in thanking those brave veterans of World War II, American, Canadian, British, Polish, Dutch, Free French, Russian, and on and on, who gave or risked their lives to rescue entire civilian populations from raw terror.

Contributors

Christina M. Sobole van der Kroon lives in Las Vegas, Nevada

Gerry Bijwaard was eight when the war began, living in Woerden. He moved to Australia in 1953, and to the USA in 1956. He was drafted into the army, got his engineering degree and worked for GE in Schenectady, New York, while earning his Master's degree. He and his wife, Patricia, live in Virginia.

Anthonia Huysman-Bamberg was seven years old at the beginning of the war, and lived in Groningen. She came to the USA with her parents in 1948. She has a son, a daughter, and two grandchildren, and lives in Buena Park, California.

Johanna Oostra was born in Scheveningen in 1933, and spent the war in The Hague. Seven years after the war she and her new husband, Peter, emigrated to Cape Town, South Africa. In 1961 they moved to the USA.

Petronella Vanderdonk was born in Culemborg. She married a Canadian soldier and settled in Yarmouth, Nova Scotia. After being widowed twice she returned to her maiden name. Petronella still lives in Yarmouth.

Ann Mons Veldhuis grew up in Zutphen. She was five when her father died in 1941, after which the family (mother and three children) moved in with her maternal grandfather, near the IJssel River. She now lives near Victoria, British Columbia.

Johanna VandenBroek was born in Westerbeek, in 1926. She came to Canada in 1955 with her husband, Martin. They live in Cardigan, Prince Edward Island, where she and her husband raised ten children. In 2005 she published a book about the war, 'When the Green Letter Comes Over'.

Ben Wind was born in 1933 in Winterswijk, but a year later the family moved to Dinxperlo. He came to Canada in 1952 and worked as a typewriter technician, later setting up his own business. Ben and his wife live in Vancouver, British, Columbia.

Bill de Groot was born in Bussum, where his family spent the war. He came to the USA in 1964, and worked as a professional and registered Mechanical Engineer. He and his wife, Lisette, have two daughters and one son. They live in Asheville, North Carolina.

Cornelia Gilbert was born in The Hague in 1939, and came to Canada with her parents and younger sister in 1957. She lives in Ottawa, Ontario.

Christine Dodenbier was born in Amsterdam but lived in Ede when the war began. She was eleven years old at the time. In 1951 she followed her fiancé to Salt Lake City where they initially settled. Later she moved to Ogden, Utah, where she still lives.

Cor Feenstra was born in Rotterdam in 1923. He spent time in five different concentration camps during the last year of the war before being liberated. In 1956 he left for the USA with his wife and two children. He worked for 31 years in Jamestown, New York as an electrician. When he retired in 1985 they moved to Florida. His wife died in 2003. Cor now lives in Kihei, Hawaii.

Elsa Abma was born in 1930 in Hillegersberg, a suburb of Rotterdam. Her family moved to Velp, near Arnhem. She met her husband in 1955 when he was on a visit to Holland after having previously emigrated to the USA. She followed him to Oregon five months later. They have four children.

Frans Dullemond was born in Delft in 1936. His family moved to the Achterhoek region in 1944. Frans came to Canada with his wife and two children in 1980, where he initially settled in Richmond, British Columbia. He now lives in Chilliwack, British Columbia.

George Hansman was twelve when the war began, living in Amsterdam. He came to Canada with his wife and two children in 1949, settling in Dauphin, Manitoba for three years where he worked as a mechanical engineer with the Canadian National Railway. They moved around in both Canada and South America over the years. He now lives in Stevensville, Ontario.

Henny Merkley grew up in Zuidwolde. She married a Canadian soldier in 1945 and followed him to Canada the following year. Her parents followed them two years later. Henny and Ken had three children. Henny lives in Thunder Bay, Ontario.

Klaas Korver was born on the island of Texel in 1934. He and his wife Nel came to Canada in 1965 with two children, and had another one later. Klaas worked in technical engineering. He and Nel live in Nepean, a suburb of Ottawa, Ontario.

Enno Reckendorf was born in 1930. He sent in his story from Hertford, North Carolina.

Hans ten Bruggenkate and his family lived in Ruurlo, Gelderland, when it was liberated on April 1, 1945. He now lives in Kingston, Ontario.

Hidde Yedema was born in Witmarsum in 1935 but grew up in Makkum, another Frisian town. He and his new wife, Nelly Bottema, came to Canada in March 1950. Their five children grew up in Cornwall, Ontario, where Hidde ran a bakery. Nelly died in 2000, and Hidde now lives in Laval, Québec with his second wife, Louise.

Henry Niezen grew up in Zwolle, Overijssel. The war started when he was sixteen. He came to Canada in 1951 with his wife. They had four children in different towns, since Henry worked in construction and moved all around British Columbia. Henry lives in Victoria, British Columbia.

Jacoba Bessey lived in Haarlem when the war began, one of four girls. Her brother Hans was born in 1941. She now lives in Regina, Saskatchewan.

Jenny Blad was born in the city of Groningen in 1937 as the oldest of six. She came to Canada in 1958 with her new husband and three words of English. She now lives in Westbank, British Columbia.

Joe Verstappen was born in St. Oedenrode. He came to Canada with his wife in 1952. They successively lived in northern Ontario, California, and Grants Pass, Oregon, where they still live. Joe always worked as a tailor and still has customers at age 82. He and his wife have two daughters, three grandchildren, and three great-grandchildren.

John Keulen was born near Chicago in 1931 to Dutch immigrants. They returned to The Netherlands when John was two years old, settling in the Frisian village of Bakhuizen. In 1948 they returned to the United States with John and his brother.

Nelia Barnfield was two years old at the beginning of the war. Her family lived in Enschede then, but moved to Leiden in 1941. She now lives in Victoria, BC.

Nina Reitsma-de Groot was born in 1942 in the city of Groningen. She and her husband came to the USA in 1967 for his studies, then spent two years in England before coming to Winnipeg, Canada in 1979. They have three sons and seven grandchildren, and have lived in Windsor, Ontario since 1986.

Lisette de Groot was born in the Dutch East Indies. When she was three her mother died and she went to stay with an aunt and uncle in Rotterdam. Her father remarried, and the family lived in Voorschoten when the war started. Lisette and her husband emigrated to Jacksonville, Florida in 1964. They retired to Asheville, North Carolina.

Michael van der Boon was born and raised in Scheveningen. During the war his family was evacuated to the Bezuidenhout section of The Hague. He makes his home in Hidden Valley Lake, CA.

Pauline Hofman was born in Amsterdam, but her family moved away from the city to be near relatives in a more rural area. She now lives in Geneva, Nevada.

Nellie van Eyk grew up in Rotterdam. She and her sister, both nurses, traveled to many different countries. Nellie moved to Nova Scotia in 1949 and married her boyfriend there within a month. They had four children but Nellie continued nursing part-time. She now lives in Cobourg, Ontario.

Susan Rombeek grew up in The Hague. She emigrated to the USA in 1967 with her husband, Edward, on the day he was discharged from the Dutch Navy. Susan worked before returning to university to get her Master's degree as counseling psychologist, and then worked as a school psychologist. She lives on Guemes Island, near Anacortes, Washington.

Robert Colyn was fourteen when the war began. He went to school in Haarlem, while his parents, in the Dutch East Indies, were interned in Japanese camps. Robert did not see them from 1939 until after the war. He married in 1951 and emigrated to Brazil. He then took a job in Akron, Ohio, where he lived until 1962. After four years back in Holland, he moved to Salinas, California.

Rita Dijkstra lives in Kamloops, British Columbia.

Ankie Bruigom was born in 1935 in Hillegom, South Holland. She came to Canada in 1959 on De Grote Beer, alone, but married in Canada. She later worked in a hospital as an activities aide. Ankie has four children and two grandchildren. She lives in Comox, British Columbia.

William Rooyakkers sent in his contribution from Albuquerque, New Mexico.

Piet Vermeulen was born 1929 in Strijen, Zuid-Holland. He came to Canada as a 19-year-old in 1948. He and his wife have four children, twelve grandchildren, and six great-grandchildren. He lives in Bowmanville, Ontario.

Katherina de Leeuw was born in The Hague and was seven when the war started. In 1958 she came to Canada with her husband and settled in Wallaceburg, Ontario where they had five children. She now lives in Chatham, Ontario.

Kees Vermeer was almost ten when the Nazis invaded Holland. In 1954 he emigrated to Canada, where he obtained a M.Sc. in Zoology from the University of British Columbia, and a PhD. from the University of Alberta. He became a research scientist for the Canadian Wildlife Service. Kees has produced numerous scientific publications and was active in various professional organizations. He lives in Sidney, British Columbia.

Hetty Wear was 21 in 1946 when she married a Canadian soldier, John Wear. She followed him to Edmonton, Alberta where she still lives. She has a daughter and two sons, several grandchildren and great-grandchildren. John died in 1999. Hetty attends monthly meetings of Edmonton war brides.

Frank VanderKley lived with his family in The Hague. He was six when the war began. He emigrated to Canada in 1953 to escape the military draft, and worked on a farm in Alberta. He later became a lawyer.

Dirk Hoogeveen was almost thirteen when The Netherlands was invaded by Germany. Dirk came to Canada with his wife in 1953 and settled in Regina.

Else Bevelander was a teenager during the war, living in The Hague. She and her husband came to Canada in 1958, where they had three children and built up a good life. They live in Willowdale, Ontario.

The Dutch in Wartime series

Book 1
Invasion

Edited by:
Tom Bijvoet

90 pages paperback
ISBN: 978-0-9868308-0-8

Book 2
Under Nazi Rule

Edited by:
Tom Bijvoet

88 pages paperback
ISBN: 978-0-9868308-3-9

Book 3
Witnessing the Holocaust

Edited by:
Tom Bijvoet

96 pages paperback
ISBN: 978-0-9868308-5-3

Book 4
Resisting Nazi Occupation

Edited by:
Anne van Arragon Hutten

108 pages paperback
ISBN: 978-0-9868308-4-6

Book 5
Tell your children about us

Edited by:
Anne van Arragon Hutten

104 pages paperback
ISBN: 978-0-9868308-6-0

Book 6
War in the Indies

Edited by:
Anne van Arragon Hutten

96 pages paperback
ISBN: 978-0-9868308-7-7

Book 7
Caught in the crossfire

Edited by:
Anne van Arragon Hutten

104 pages paperback
ISBN: 978-0-9868308-8-4

Book 8
The Hunger Winter

Edited by:
Tom Bijvoet
&
Anne van Arragon Hutten

110 pages paperback
ISBN: 978-0-9868308-9-1

Keep your series complete:
order on-line at mokeham.com
or contact Mokeham Publishing.

If you are interested in
The Netherlands
and its people,
try **DUTCH** *the magazine.*

Go to
www.mokeham.com/dutchthemag
for more information.